The Magic of
OLD TRACTORS

To read without reflecting is like eating without digesting.

Edmund Burke

The Magic of
OLD TRACTORS

Ian M Johnston

NH
NEW
HOLLAND

This book is dedicated to the memory
of Bert and 'Rita' Johnston,
and Harold and Ethel Davis.

First published in Australia in 2004 by
New Holland Publishers (Australia) Pty Ltd
Sydney • Auckland • London • Cape Town

14 Aquatic Drive Frenchs Forest NSW 2086 Australia
218 Lake Road Northcote Auckland New Zealand
86 Edgware Road London W2 2EA United Kingdom
80 McKenzie Street Cape Town 8001 South Africa

National Library of Australia Cataloguing-in-Publication Data:
Johnston, Ian M, 1935– .
The magic of old tractors.

Includes index.
ISBN 1 74110 002 X.

1. Tractors—History. 2. Farm tractors—History. 3.
Antique and classic tractors—History. I. Title.

629.2252

Publishing Manager: Robynne Millward
Project Editor: Karen Gee
Designer: Karlman Roper
Production Manager: Linda Bottari
Reproduction: Kolorart Graphics, Sydney
Printer: Leefung-Asco, China

10 9 8 7 6 5 4 3 2
This book is typeset in ElegantGaramondBT 11pt.

Every effort has been made to trace the original source material in this book.
Where the attempt has been unsuccessful, the publishers would be pleased to hear
from the copyright holder to rectify any omission.

Front cover: Massey Harris 102 Senior (Shaw Collection, Tasmania)
Back cover: Landini L25 advertisement, courtesy Landini, Fabbrico, Italy.

Contents

Introduction 6

Measurements used in this book 9

A word about kerosene fuel 10

So what *is* the magic of old tractors? 11

Horsepower and drawbar pull 16

Legend of the Big 4 22

The remarkable Saunderson Type A 28

The Rumely Oil Pull classics 34

The Moline Universal 38

The industrial cousins 42

Lightweights 51

Leave it to Ludwig 70

Heavyweights 74

The early Marshalls 90

Orenstein & Koppel S32K 98

The big semidiesels 101

The BMC Mini, a brilliant tractor—nearly 120

T Herbert Morrell and the Oliver Super 55 124

The Alios Murr story 129

Tractor engine designs of the 1950s 138

The row croppers 148

Renault 3042 155

Evolution of the David Brown Cropmaster 159

The Burly tractors—and me 165

Spare parts 173

Acknowledgments 188

Index 189

Introduction

With four books and several hundred magazine articles behind me, all relating to classic tractors, it is often suggested that there can be nothing left for me to write on this subject. Sometimes I wish there were an element of accuracy in this observation. I would then be free to concentrate fully upon the old tractors in my collection, some of which are still awaiting their turn for restoration. The truth is, there is so much more about which I can write concerning these clanking old machines, I am obliged to agonise over what to leave out!

Admittedly, the whole job of writing *The Magic of Old Tractors* could have been rendered less demanding had I simply chosen to rearrange others' words and write columns of specifications and text liberally sprinkled with tedious data. But with over half a century of practical tractor and farming experience under my belt, I am in the fortunate position of being able to 'tell it how it was'. As I write about a specific tractor, in most instances I am able to recall its sounds, its idiosyncrasies and most of all its character.

Additionally, I am able to recollect, with a fair degree of accuracy, the yarns recounted to me in my youth by oldtimers. They told me of the days when steam power was replaced by the tractor. This occurred in the early 20th century when they themselves were youngsters, a time when Edward VII was King of England and Theodore Roosevelt President of the USA.

I am also privileged to be the recipient of constant streams of classic tractor information arriving by email, fax, letter and telephone from contacts around the world. Some of the items constitute mere snippets of trivia, others are in the form of graphics with descriptions, but occasionally material of monumental historic and technical significance arrives upon my desk. Information is also unearthed as a result of spending several months each year travelling, often to remote places, researching and authenticating historic tractor data.

Accordingly, being the custodian of all this classic tractor material, there is a responsibility for me to share it with the rapidly expanding legions of tractor enthusiasts and clubs around the world. I have endeavoured to shoehorn

into the pages of *The Magic of Old Tractors* a broad cross-section of this information. Countless facts are either examined in-depth or mentioned in passing. It is possible that some issues may remain open for discussion or criticism; no doubt my peers will alert me if such be the case.

Invitations to serve as a judge or guest speaker at tractor rallies ensure I remain in touch with fellow enthusiasts. This is important to me, as I am able to obtain an appreciation of the expectations they have for the contents of my future books.

Somewhat egotistically perhaps, I have included a scattering of personal narratives, which I believe will assist in the portrayal of the tractor scene as it was half a century ago.

Over 300 graphics have been carefully selected to illustrate the tractors reviewed. I confess to a few having appeared in my previous works, however the majority are being published for the first time. Care has been taken with the accuracy of colour reproduction. If known, the name of the owner of each tractor pictured is credited in the accompanying captions. Please note that I have, on occasion, included photos of indifferent quality. This is on account of their historical significance and the contribution they make to the book.

Not surprisingly, there are some tractor makes that are not included. These have either been mentioned in my previous works or perhaps will appear in the future. Others of particular interest are being reviewed again, but in greater detail.

When I use the term 'classic' or 'classic era', I am referring to the first sixty years of tractor production.

You are now invited to share my nostalgic world of spanners, grease and exhaust smoke and become acquainted (or re-acquainted, if you're an old tractor man like me) with *The Magic of Old Tractors*.

Ian M Johnston

A 1935 John Deere BR owned and restored by
Bart Cushing. Photographed in a forest clearing
in New Hampshire, USA. *(Courtesy B Cushing)*

The Magic of Old Tractors

Measurements used in this book

All performance and dimensional measurements are given in the terminology employed by the manufacturers of the particular model being discussed. Therefore, some imperial measurements intentionally appear with decimal points in accordance with those provided by the manufacturer or test authority. For those who may be unfamiliar with some of the measurements employed, a table of conversions appears below.

IMPERIAL TO METRIC	METRIC TO IMPERIAL
Length	
1in = 25.4mm	1cm = 0.394in
1ft = 30.5cm	1m = 3.28ft
1yd = 0.914m	1m = 1.09yd
1 mile = 1.61km	1km = 0.621 mile
Mass	
1oz = 28.3g	1g = 0.0353oz
1lb = 454g	1kg = 2.2lb
1 ton = 1.02t	1t = 0.984 ton
Area	
1 in2 = 6.45cm^2	1cm2 = 0.155in^2
1ft2 = 929cm^2	1m2 = 10.8ft^2
1yd2 = 0.836m^2	1m2 = 1.20yd^2
1ac = 0.405ha	1ha = 2.47ac
1 square mile = 2.59km^2	1km^2 = 0.386 square mile
Volume	
1in3 = 16.4cm^3	1cm3 = 0.061in^3
1ft3 = 0.0283m^3	1m3 = 35.3ft^3
1yd3 = 0.765m^3	1m3 = 1.31yd^3
1fl oz = 28.4ml	1ml = 0.0352fl oz
1pt = 568ml	1L = 1.76pt
1gal = 4.55L	1m^3 = 220gal
1 acre foot = 1.23Ml	1Ml = 0.811 acre foot
Pressure	
1psi = 6.89kPa	1kPa = 0.145psi
Power	
1hp = 0.746kW	1kW = 1.34hp

A word about kerosene fuel

Since the inception of tractors at the beginning of the 20th century, kerosene (paraffin) was offered as a cheap alternative to petrol (gasoline). Being lower in the refining process, kerosene cost less to produce and therefore made economic sense for use as a tractor fuel in a conventional internal combustion engine. However, being less volatile than petrol, it first had to be heated (in order to vaporise and thus form an explosive gaseous mixture) when drawn through the inlet manifold into the combustion chamber.

It was therefore always necessary to start a kerosene-fuelled tractor engine initially on petrol and run it for some minutes, enabling the exhaust gases to warm the 'hot box' section of the inlet manifold. When this was sufficiently hot the petrol was turned off and the kerosene tap opened. The kerosene was then heated as it passed through the hot box and consequently vaporised. The engine then ran on preheated kerosene.

Prior to stopping the engine, it was usual to switch off the kerosene flow and revert to petrol. By doing so, the carburettor contained petrol ready for the next day's start. The saving to farmers by using kerosene, which cost around half that of petrol, could be quite considerable. A heavyweight, fuel-guzzling tractor such as the Case LA could easily consume four gallons of fuel per hour.

Collectors of old petrol–kerosene tractors today are often concerned about the unavailability of power kerosene. They are worried that their tractor engine, designed to operate on kerosene fuel, may suffer damage if continually run on petrol. In fact, petrol is more kind to an engine than kerosene. The latter is an abrasive fuel which is likely to pollute the lubricating oil. This can occur if the engine has not reached the optimum operating temperature and some of the kerosene therefore remains unburned, finding its way into the sump past the piston rings.

In the days when petrol–kerosene-fuelled tractors were in common use, it was standard practice each morning, after the oil in the sump had settled overnight and the contaminating kerosene had risen to the upper layer of the oil, for around one quart to be drawn off the upper level of the oil through a special discharge screw in the side of the sump. A replacement quart of fresh oil would then be added to raise the level to the required amount.

Additionally, the engine oil of a petrol–kerosene-fuelled tractor had to be routinely changed every fifty hours, as opposed to every 100 hours if running only on petrol. A contemporary vintage tractor owner can therefore relax in the knowledge that the potential life of the petrol–kerosene engine is being prolonged by being run on petrol only.

To avoid confusion it should be noted that 'paraffin', 'lamp oil' and 'vaporising oil' are alternative terms used broadly to describe kerosene.

In the USA during the 1930s and 1940s, kerosene was often loosely referred to as 'distillate', which was a variable and poorly defined fuel having similar properties to kerosene. Paradoxically, in some parts of the world today the term 'distillate' is a trade name for the diesel fuel commonly run in diesel engines.

So what *is* the magic of old tractors?

Why is it that some grown men and women develop an attachment to old tractors that can ripen into a lifelong passionate obsession? What precisely is the magic ingredient, emanating from those ancient pieces of ironmongery, that is capable of converting a normal well-adjusted mind into a state of consuming preoccupation?

These are questions frequently pondered by 'unenlightened' normal mortals when confronted with a rusty relic being fussed over by a devoted owner, as might a delicate child be pampered by a caring parent. Conversely tractor lovers, when asked about their *affair de coeur,* can only feel saddened that such questions should have to be asked. A feeling of pity for the enquirer is rarely accompanied by a response.

Frankly, there can be no satisfactory or conclusive answer. There is no relevant text book to consult and even that font of all knowledge, the computer, would likely suffer a terminal relapse if pressed hard for the perfect answer. In the event that some brave soul did attempt to unravel the mystery surrounding the magic of old tractors, then that stalwart would have to include the term 'character' in their response. One thing is definite: old tractors certainly reek of character!

The individual attributes of vintage cars, trucks, buses and even of old aeroplanes, motor bikes and bicycles were discovered years ago. Museums, dedicated to these varied modes of transportation, have existed for half a century or more. But old tractors, with their abundance of idiosyncratic character, were only largely first discovered and appreciated during the later part of the 20th century.

This quite extraordinary phenomenon of the awareness of old tractors has erupted in Australia, Britain, Europe, Ireland, New Zealand, North America and South Africa. Untold numbers of decaying hulks have been rescued from their places of abandonment and now repose in elegant retirement within the caring hands of their doting new owners.

Vintage tractor clubs are springing up everywhere, in both rural and outer urban communities. Classic tractor events, including rallies, treks, meets, tractor pulls and reunions are held somewhere on any given weekend. They are attended by a rapidly growing legion of exhibitors and onlookers who flock from one show to the next.

Originally, classic tractor events consisted of static displays, which were interesting enough. But by the new millennium they had evolved into visually exciting spectacles of old tractors participating in a variety of imaginative games and competitions. These include both high-speed and slow racing, balancing, blindfold navigating and timed cranking and dashing. Sophisticated, variably weighted sleds were constructed for comparing the pulling ability of different makes and models.

Today, these tractor events have developed into highly competitive yet fun activities to which throngs of enthusiasts converge each weekend. Some exhibitors and spectators routinely travel hundreds (and even thousands) of kilometres to attend shows, particularly in the USA, where road travel is easy on the magnificent network of interstate highways.

Collectors of old tractors usually aim to restore their treasures to as-new condition. This can be a time consuming and expensive exercise; quite frequently a set of new tyres will cost more than the price paid for the tractor. Some enthusiasts are content to simply get a machine running sweetly and ignore the costly cosmetics. Certainly, a classic in its original 'working clothes' has an appeal all of its own and can be admired just as much as a unit that has been treated to a fresh coat of paint.

Regrettably, there is a minority of classic tractor folk who are not committed collectors in the true sense. They are hoarders! Such hoarders arrive at auction sales and generally manage to outbid dedicated enthusiasts. Their new purchases are carted home, where they are parked out in the open, under a tree, with all the other relics that are simply rusting away. Hoarders seem to be unaware that the worst place to park an old tractor is under a tree. All trees drip corrosive material, plus drop seeds, pollen and of course leaves. If challenged about their intentions, there is a standard reply stating that the tractors will be restored 'one day'!

The evidence points to the contrary. A hoarder's tractors are unlikely to ever be restored. This is a shame because old tractors, once acquired, must be housed and protected from the elements. Fuels, oils and water should be changed and it is desirable that a 'stuck' engine be freed with a degree of urgency. A tractor falling into the uncaring hands of a hoarder means one less to be preserved for posterity.

Wittingly or unwittingly, genuine tractor collectors perform a service to their country—they are doing their bit to safeguard items of national heritage. Yes, old tractors are indeed heritage objects. They represent an era long gone and are a living history of the development of mechanised

The 'blindfold navigation' competition is performed with a bucket over the operator's head, which not only cuts out vision but also causes disorientation. The challenge is to steer to, and stop the tractor at, a marker on the ground. Mick Pettith and his International McCormick Super AWD6 are regular competitors in this class. *(Courtesy U Schultz)*

farming. They are also a testimony to those whose visionary minds created them. Had the farm tractor not evolved, the great food-producing nations such as Australia, Canada, the USA and Russia could not have developed their vast plains of golden grain.

Collectors can take pride, and are entitled to a feeling of fulfilment and achievement, in their endeavours to preserve their country's national heritage. Thank goodness for these tractor lovers who have discovered this fascination and magic. Without their dedication, future generations would be deprived the experience of gazing in wonderment upon old classic tractors and the joy of hearing them clanking around the arena at a vintage tractor rally.

As to a clinically precise definition of 'magic' as it relates to old tractors—who cares!

At the drop of the flag, the two competitors run a distance of 20 metres to their tractors, then furiously crank the Massey Harris 30 and the International Farmall A into life, jump onto the seat and race for the line. First to arrive wins and progresses to the next heat. *(Courtesy M Daw)*

Some vintage tractor owners take great pride in recreating the actual working conditions that occurred over half a century ago. Evan Lanyon, a John Deere enthusiast, has not only restored his 1948 John Deere Model AR, but also a matching John Deere 402 disc plough. Both units are in as-new condition and make a fine picture as they turn over the stubble. *(Courtesy L Lanyon)*

Vintage tractor treks originated in New Zealand and are now gaining in popularity elsewhere. Pictured is a group of trekkers crossing Dingo Creek in Wingham, Australia. *(Courtesy M Blake)*

A 1949 Australian-built KL Bulldog delights the crowd as it outpulls a Mack truck. It was considered that the 1-cylinder, 40hp Bulldog would have no chance against the 8-cylinder, 280hp Mack. But in a 'best of three' the Bulldog won two out of three. *(Courtesy M Pettith)*

Bob Radnidge has chosen to leave his 1937 Case Model C in its original working clothes. *(Courtesy M Blake)*

The magic of classic tractors was even apparent in 1925, as evidenced in the photo above, showing throngs of spectators lining a street in Munich, Germany. The occasion was a procession celebrating the opening of the new Munich Machinery Museum on 7 May of that year. The reason for the Lanz Bulldog tractors pulling a trailer (upon which is mounted an aircraft—could it be a Gotha?) is unclear, but it certainly was a crowd-pleaser. *(Courtesy J Deere/Lanz Archives, Mannheim)*

B and T Batchelor elected to carry out a complete mechanical and cosmetic restoration of their ultra-rare 1918 Ruggles & Parson 12-20.

Horsepower and drawbar pull

From the very early days of tractors, farmers have been bombarded with an array of tractor performance figures, provided initially by the manufacturers and later by various testing authorities. These can prove confusing and often meaningless to the less technically inclined. This chapter aims to unravel some of the complexities with which farmers were faced.

THE BASICS

Possibly the most basic, and least scientific, of these were figures advertised by some of America's pioneer tractor manufacturers at the beginning of the 20th century. They simply stated that a particular model of tractor had the ability to haul a plough which would normally be pulled by a specified number of horses. This rating was referred to as 'number of horses replaced'. Unscientific, maybe—but farmers felt comfortable with, and could relate to, this type of down-to-earth analogy and would use it as the basis for their decision on which tractor to purchase.

There were, however, more scientific horsepower (hp) ratings for early tractor owners or potential buyers to also consider. It was common practice to allocate a model type to a specific tractor, defined by drawbar hp and belt hp. For example, in 1912 the Avery Power Machinery Company of Peoria, Illinois, introduced its model 12-25. The reference to '12-25' indicated it produced 12 drawbar hp and 25 belt hp. Interestingly, the number of horses replaced was rated as being five to six.

In the period 1920–1960 a more meaningful and practical measurement of a tractor's ability to pull a soil-engaging implement was drawbar pull. This figure was measured in pounds or kilograms, but had to be related to the speed at which the pull was achieved. On its own, drawbar pull represented only half the equation.

The following example will serve to explain this point: A petrol–kerosene-fuelled John Deere Model D and a diesel-fuelled International McCormick WD6 each returned a maximum drawbar pull of approximately 4800lbs, when tested at The University of Nebraska Engineering Department tractor test facility in the 1940s.

But the John Deere achieved its pull at 2.68mph whilst the International produced its maximum pull at only 1.97mph. At first glance the slight difference in speed may appear irrelevant, but under field conditions the D would likely outpull the WD6.

The term 'likely' is used as two other factors have to be considered. It was customary during the testing of the pneumatic tyred tractors (which first appeared in the early 1930s) for manufacturers to add ballast to the rear wheels and/or axles in order to provide the tractor with additional weight, thus a better grip. By doing so, a higher but artificial drawbar pull could be recorded. Therefore it was significant for a farmer analysing the test results, to note that the John Deere D was laden with an additional 2064lbs in order to return the 4830lbs pull. However, the International McCormick WD6 was provided with no less than 2726lbs of additional ballast to record its 4806lbs pull!

The final factor requiring scrutiny was the examination of percentage of wheel slip measured during maximum pull. Under test conditions, the John Deere experienced 14.97 per cent slip and the International, despite its greater amount of ballast, registered 18.03 per cent. It should be noted that in field conditions it is normal for a wheeled tractor under load to return a wheel slippage of between 5 and 7 per cent. Between these parameters the tractor is working efficiently with a well-balanced load. A figure beyond 15 per cent is considered unsatisfactory and will result in wastage of fuel and excessive tyre wear.

A common adage used by farmers for assessing a tractor's wheel slip was, 'If you can see the wheels spinning, then it's not working properly.' This old-fashioned assessment was based on the fact that a wheel slippage of less than 5 per cent is almost impossible to detect visually.

Despite producing nearly identical drawbar pulls under test conditions, the John Deere D and International McCormick WD6 were in fact totally differing design concepts and under field conditions performed quite differently. Accordingly, if a prospective buyer had narrowed the choice down to between the two, they would have been wise to arrange a comparative demonstration on their own farm with their own implements. All the technical mumbo jumbo in the world would not have proved so decisive as a practical hands-on field test!

This advertisement for Avery tractors was featured widely in American rural journals around 1912. Common with many early tractors, the Avery had exposed gears. The assault upon the gear facings from grit and mud caused rapid and excessive wear. Later models had gear trains protected by covers or located internally within sealed transmission housings.

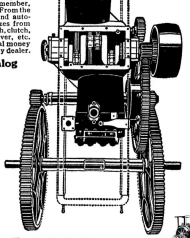

A meticulously restored John Deere D. The John Deere D was in production from 1923 until 1953, an all-time 30-year record for any tractor model. It was also the only John Deere to be of unit construction (i.e. without a frame or chassis, the engine and transmission housings being bolted together to form a single rigid unit). The two cylinders were positioned horizontally, side by side, facing forward. The 2-cylinder design was retained in all John Deere models until the 4- and 6-cylinder units were introduced in 1960. During the production life of the Model D it was given several upgrades and the final version (pictured) proved an outstanding tractor despite its inherited old technology, which included chain-driven final drives. Owned by Brian Sainsbury.

THE COMPLEXITY OF HORSEPOWER CALCULATIONS

The term horsepower was first adopted by Scotsman James Watt (1736–1819). In a practical test he found that a draught horse, walking at the rate of 2½mph, could draw 150lbs of coal (by means of a rope fed through a pulley) vertically at the rate of 220 feet per minute. This equated, so he determined, to 33 000lbs raised vertically to the height of 1 foot in one minute.

The above basic (and perhaps questionable) horsepower formula has spawned a range of hp ratings. Those having a relevance to tractors are as follows:

Indicated hp is of little interest to farmers, as it is purely a mathematical figure indicating the power theoretically developed within the cylinder(s) of the engine.

Brake hp is the power developed by an engine at specific revolutions per minute (rpm), available at the flywheel and measured by the resistance offered by a brake.

Belt hp is the actual hp produced at the belt pulley and is usually less than the brake hp due to frictional losses through the gearing. This rating was important in the era when most tractors were routinely used to drive machines (threshers, balers, pumps etc.) via a flat endless belt from the tractor's belt pulley.

Power take off (pto) hp has replaced the belt hp ratings in modern times. Power take off (pto) shafts now do the job of the endless belt and are used commonly for supplying energy to attached front or rear implements. This measurement is of the hp actually available at the pto shaft and is the figure favoured as being the most relevant by today's tractor manufacturers.

RAC hp, the Royal Automobile Club hp, is of little relevance to power capability as it was a calculation used by the British government to levy tax on vehicles and was calculated as follows: cylinder bore^2 x number of cylinders x 0.4.

Added to the above is the need to know if the hp in question is *maximum* or *rated*.

Maximum is determined as being the peak figure achieved for only a brief duration.

Rated is a figure that can be sustained over a given duration.

Mick Pettith's 1954 International McCormick Super AWD6 is shown going through its paces at a vintage tractor pull competition. Note the extra ballast added to the rear axles to provide additional weight, and thus grip, in order to increase the drawbar pull of the tractor. The Super AWD6 was manufactured at International Harvester's Australian Geelong plant (the letter 'A' indicates the Australian manufacture). The Super series was introduced in 1952 and was a development of the original WD6, first produced in the USA in 1940. The original (1940) engine developed 34.7 belt hp and, although being a diesel unit, was first started on petrol, employing a magneto system, before switching over to diesel and the associated higher compression ratio.

A COMPARISON OF HORSEPOWER CHARACTERISTICS

It is interesting to compare the individual performances of the following similarly powered tractors and to note the number of horses replaced.

1920 Emerson Brantingham Q 12-20

The Emerson Brantingham Q 12-20 was powered by a 4-cylinder engine with the cylinders cast in pairs. Lubrication was by splash feed. As a result, if the tractor was operated for any length of time on a lean the system failed to supply an adequate amount of oil to the engine's vital components. In order to overcome this problem the front-wheel track was wider than that of the rear, so that when mouldboard ploughing only the offside front wheel ran in the furrow and the tractor remained level. The Model Q was considered one of the more reliable tractors of the time.

> **1920 Emerson Brantingham Q 12-20**
>
> **Number of horses replaced:** 6–7
> **Max. belt hp:** 27.3
> **Max. drawbar hp:** 15.55
> **Max. drawbar pull:** 3022lbs at 2.18mph
> **Engine:** own

An Emerson Brantingham Q 12-20 owned by prominent grain farmer Dan Ehlerding of Jamestown, Ohio.

1920 Gray S 18-36

Number of horses replaced: 6–8
Maximum belt hp: 32.2
Maximum drawbar hp: 19.5
Maximum drawbar pull: 3390lbs
At mph: 2.12
Engine: Waukesha

1920 Gray S 18-36

The Gray S 18-36 was built in Minneapolis, Minnesota, by the Gray Tractor Company and powered by a cross-mounted Waukesha 4-cylinder petrol–kerosene engine. When introduced in 1918 it was possibly the world's first custom-built orchard tractor. The corrugated iron overhead panelling was reminiscent of a hen house, but did serve to protect the branches of fruit trees as the tractor worked along the rows. The full-width driving wheel was actually built in two sections and brandished spiked grips. The examples illustrated are two of only a handful of remaining Gray tractors. The upper photo was taken at the Western Development Museum, Saskatchewan, Canada. The lower photo was taken at the Reynold's Alberta Museum, Wetaskawin, Alberta.

1925 Heider Rock Island 15-27

The Heider Manufacturing Company of Carroll, Iowa, entered the tractor business in 1911 when it introduced the Heider Friction Drive tractor. In 1916 the Rock Island Plow Company of Rock Island, Illinois, acquired the Heider Manufacturing Company and continued to produce and market tractors under the Heider name. The 15-27 was powered by the same 4-cylinder Waukesha engine as fitted to the Gray 18-36. The variances in performance figures between the two tractors is the result of differing gearing, weight, engine rpm and wheel design. The Heider pictured is on display at the Barr Colony Heritage Cultural Centre, Lloydminster, Canada.

1925 Heider Rock Island 15-27

Number of horses replaced: 7–9
Maximum belt hp: 30.0
Maximum drawbar hp: 21.54
Maximum drawbar pull: 3302lbs
At mph: 2.45
Engine: Waukesha (friction drive)

Legend of the Big 4

In these modern times, when we are surrounded by technological advances, it may be easy to imagine ourselves as being more intelligent than our forebears. For after all, are we not masters of the computer chip? Voyages into space are so regular they warrant only a brief mention in the media. We can transplant hearts, replace hips and knees and perform other miracles of medical science. However, such technological and scientific marvels did not simply occur overnight— they evolved, thanks to the pioneering work of experts in such fields. The same applies to modern computer-designed tractors. They didn't just happen.

Merely a century of time has elapsed since the first embryonic, rudimentary tractors were conceived—and from a historic perspective, a century is a very short space of time indeed.

The early tractor pioneers were men of great vision. Giants among them included Dan Albone, Henry Ford, John Froelich, Alfred H McDonald, to mention just a few. These men each shared a common challenge; by virtue of the fact that they were the first, they each had to commence with a clean sheet of paper and create their own interpretation of a tractor. There were no precedents to which they could refer. There were no guidelines in text books and there was certainly no computer software to provide assistance with their projects.

Not surprisingly therefore, many ideas were trialled and rejected. Metallurgy was in itself a little-understood science that was going through a phase of exploration and discovery. Commonly, tractor components were crafted over an anvil in a blacksmith's shop. Heavy iron was still used in strategic areas where steel, with its extra strength, could have resulted in lighter weight. The technique of stress relieving was not practised until much later.

Early American tractors could almost be referred to as hybrid steam traction engines. Obviously, the steam boiler and associated mechanisms had been replaced by the internal combustion engine. But girder frames, open gears and large diameter steel wheels remained. The power units were generally single- or twin-cylinder stationary engines simply mounted upon the tractor frame and coupled to the transmission by chain, gear or friction engagement. Tractors that conformed to this design included: the 1898 Huber, powered by a single-cylinder engine with a heated platinum wire in place of a spark plug; the 1901 Kindred Haines, with its 200rpm horizontal single-cylinder engine; and the 1904 Dissinger with a similar engine to the Haines, plus several other crude contraptions. It is generally agreed that by 1906 there were ten companies in the USA fully committed to manufacturing tractors, plus an additional unknown number experimenting with prototypes.

One of the first American tractors to be powered by a custom-built tractor engine emerged as a prototype in 1904. It was the brainchild of farmer–engineer DM Hartsough. Whilst the frame and drive train conformed with the usual practice of the day (i.e. steam traction engine related components), the engine was a complete break from the traditional 1- or 2-cylinder designs. Hartsough had built a 4-cylinder overhead valve unit of massive proportions. Many of its design features are now incorporated in modern heavy duty engines.

Hartsough named his tractor the Big 4. The new tractor created a deal of interest in farming and engineering circles, as it represented a radical breakthrough in tractor development. There was little to criticise, as Hartsough's creation proved powerful, smooth and reliable.

A financier named Patrick Lyons could see considerable potential in the uniqueness of the Big 4, and in 1906 he joined with Hartsough in establishing the

Transit Thresher Company of Minneapolis, for the purpose of manufacturing the tractor. The new company made much publicity of its claim that it was the first and largest volume producer of 4-cylinder petrol-powered tractors. In 1908 the company changed its name to the Gas Traction Company.

Canadian farmers found that they too had virgin prairie to break open and the Big 4 was an ideal tractor for the purpose. Even in far off South Africa and Australia there was a demand for this type of heavy machinery. The main factor restricting sales of the Big 4 into these countries was its relatively high cost coupled with ocean freight charges.

The Emerson Brantingham Implement Company, founded in 1852 in Rockford, Illinois, had been watching the progress of the Big 4 tractor. During a period of expansion in 1912 the company took over a number of organisations, including the Gas Traction Company—and the Big 4.

In 1913 the new owners of the Big 4 briefly introduced an additional model. Remarkably, it was even larger than the standard Big 4. Designated the Model 45, it was powered by a massive 6-cylinder engine. The machine weighed 23 000lbs (10 455kg) but in fact was overly big and cumbersome and was discontinued after only two years. It is likely that the 6-cylinder Big 4 Model 45 was purely the result of Emerson Brantingham's unsuccessful endeavour to gain kudos by producing a larger tractor than either of its main opposition companies, Aultman Taylor and Minneapolis. Emerson Brantingham continued to manufacture the Big 4 until 1916.

The Emerson Brantingham Implement Company prospered and produced a diverse range of advanced design tractors. These included smaller horsepower versions of the Big 4. However in 1928 the company succumbed to a takeover bid by JI Case Company of Racine, Wisconsin.

1910 specifications of Gas Traction Co. Big 4-30
Manufacturer: Transit Thresher Co. (1906-1908), Gas Traction Co. (1908-1912), Emerson Brantingham Implement Co. (1912-1916)
Country of origin: USA
Period of manufacture: 1906–1916
Engine make: own
Engine type: 4-cyl. ohv
Cooling: water
Bore & stroke: 6.5 x 8in
Hp: 60 brake
Rpm: 550
Piston speed: 733ft per minute
Fuel tank capacity: 51 gallons
Water tank capacity: 81 gallons
Drive wheels: diameter 8ft
Gear speeds: Low—2 mph; high—3 mph
Weight: 17 500lbs

An Emerson Brantingham Big 4-30. The tractor was recovered from a grazing property, where it had been abandoned half a century previously. Many of its components had been purloined over the decades and replacements had to be remanufactured, often without the original example from which to copy. Owned by Norm Johnston.

A TRACTOR TALE

Some years ago, whilst carrying out research at a farm machinery museum in Canada, to my good fortune I was introduced to a very special old-timer. This octogenarian had come to the museum to spend the day teaching a couple of staff members the correct operating procedures of an early Big 4 tractor.

I learned that at the beginning of every summer, elderly volunteers were collected from their places of retirement and transported each day for a week to supervise the starting of the museum's early prairie tractors that had been mothballed and warehoused for the winter.

Prior to the long, bitter winter months, the cooling system of each tractor had to be drained to avoid the water freezing and cracking the engine block. In the summer it was then necessary to replenish each tractor with water (commonly 80 to 100 gallons). All lubricating tanks and sumps also had to be drained and refilled. During this operation the tractors were thoroughly serviced and checked.

When all was ready, the elderly volunteers, who had been overseeing and assisting the work, then cranked the big machines into life and trundled them out into the sunshine, where they remained on display until the autumn.

Apparently, around the time of my visit a Big 4 had been proving difficult to start. This was causing problems as it was required, along with the other tractors, to take part in occasional parades around the museum's extensive grounds. So my newfound friend had been summoned to rectify the problem.

In the afternoon I happened to sit beside him at a long table in the staff canteen, where we were provided with steaming cups of coffee sweetened with maple syrup. Although I cannot recall his name, I remember he was as thin as a young spruce, yet his face and hands had crinkled skin, giving him the appearance of a gnarled, ancient oak. But it was his eyes I shall never forget. They danced and sparkled as if he was about to embark upon a life of laughter and adventure.

Like all old-timers, he had some fascinating tales to tell. This was the reason I had travelled to Canada—to obtain first-hand experiences of early mechanised farming practices, particularly relating to the primitive dinosaurs of the tractor world. No books, documents or archival material can substitute for hearing it as it was, from someone who was there! I found it a moving encounter listening to and absorbing his teenage experiences with a Big 4. We were both transported back in time to a world of oil lamps and hard toil, but also gentleness.

He told of his father who, following a succession of good harvests, had invested in a Big 4 in 1916. The arrival of the new tractor by rail, from the Canadian assembly works in Winnipeg, had indeed been a red letter day. The very next morning it was fuelled up and the Cockshutt plough attached to the drawbar. The big tractor was then ready to prove its worth.

Owing to a wet start to the season, my elderly friend recalled, it was necessary during the first month to continue working the tractor with its trailing plough well into the night, providing the moon was amenable. An elevated bench seat with supporting back rest was installed, enabling him to be seated rather than having to remain standing all through the long night, for it was *his* task to drive the tractor during the night shift. Fortunately, the Big 4 was equipped with an optional self-steering device, which he said worked surprisingly well and relieved him of the necessity of constantly monitoring the big tractor's progress along the furrow.

The old-timer recalled how one bright moonlight night, when he was at the controls of The Big 4, he had trouble remaining awake and alert. This seemed extraordinary to me, considering the noise and jarring of the big iron-wheeled machine. But he explained that the rich arable soil was soft, therefore the ride was comparatively smooth. The 4-cylinder engine only ran at a little over 500rpm and could, he assured me, have a lulling, hypnotic effect after several hours at the controls. He started to chuckle and his merry eyes glazed over as he recounted how he had actually dozed off into a deep sleep whilst the huge tractor rumbled on into the night, dutifully following the guide wheel extending ahead in the furrow.

Cranking the Emerson Brantingham Big 4 is not a job for the faint-hearted. Two assistants check fuel and ignition, while the owner, Norm Johnston, prepares to swing the massive engine into life.

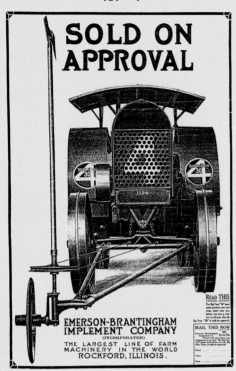

SOLD ON APPROVAL

EMERSON-BRANTINGHAM
IMPLEMENT COMPANY
(INCORPORATED)
THE LARGEST LINE OF FARM
MACHINERY IN THE WORLD
ROCKFORD, ILLINOIS.

An advertisement featured in the 1913 magazine *Gas Power*. The Big 4 is shown complete with the optional automatic steering device. The single wheel was designed to run in the ploughed furrow and thus steer the tractor without the necessity for the operator's constant attention. The device proved popular as forward vision from the driving position was severely restricted. *(Courtesy Don Beaty)*

The headland of the field happened to coincide with a kink in the dirt road which led the short distance into town. Along the edge of the road ran a shallow ditch, and into the ditch went the guide wheel. The tractor, with its sleeping operator at the controls, *headed for town!*

At this stage my octogenarian friend paused. He chuckled again and then continued. It was important, he reminded me, that I should not lose sight that all this took place in 1916. His local town, like most small, isolated Canadian townships of the period, could boast only a dirt road through its centre. Main Street had been designed for horse wagons and was lined with raised wooden sidewalks with hitch rails for the horses.

Following another bout of cackling he described to me how he was abruptly shocked into consciousness when the Big 4 came to a sudden stop. The exhaust note of the engine changed to a labouring protest and, despite the tractor's progress now being halted, the big driving wheels continued to turn. He looked around wildly and it took a second or two for him to register the appalling sight which greeted him. By now my old-timer was gasping with fits of laughter as he attempted to describe the scene of total devastation confronting him.

Apparently the huge tractor, with its broad plough, had progressed inexorably into town. It had churned its way the full length of Main Street, demolishing sidewalks, hitching rails and the barber's pole, and had finally been brought to a stop when it encountered the newly erected bandstand at the top end of the street. Recovering from his initial shock, the young driver, with considerable presence of mind, grabbed the clutch lever and killed the ignition.

That was the last I heard of the almost unbelievable tale of events that had taken place so long ago. The old-timer had collapsed into a state of wheezing chuckles and coughing as his mind remained focused on that fateful night.

Did I believe the story? Yes I did. Certainly now, after a few years, it does seem a little far-fetched. But when I recall the intensity of the old man's emotions as his mind travelled back in time, I believe I was greatly privileged to have been given the opportunity of sharing a very special memory.

Emerson Brantingham Implement Co.

1831 Ralph Emerson born Andover, Massachusetts.

1852 Emerson becomes major shareholder of John H Manny & Co. (harvesting equipment manufacturer).

1853 Manny name changed to Emerson Manufacturing Co.

1895 Emerson introduces patented Emerson plough.

1909 Emerson joins forces with Charles S Brantingham to create Emerson Brantingham Co.

1912 Emerson Brantingham Co. embarks on major expansion program and acquires Gas Traction Co., Minnesota (including Big 4 tractor works in Winnipeg, Canada), Geiser Manufacturing Co. in Pennsylvania, Reeves and Co. in Indiana, and Rockford Engineering Works, Illinois.

1913 New Big 4 Model 45 with 6-cyl. engine introduced.

1914 Death of Ralph Emerson.

1916 Production of Big 4 tractors discontinued. Other EB models continued.

1926 Emerson Brantingham 12-20 tractors imported into Australia by AH McDonald and Co.

1928 Emerson Brantingham acquired by JI Case Company. Production of all Reeves and Emerson Brantingham tractors discontinued.

An Emerson Brantingham Big 4 pulling three ploughs, circa 1913, somewhere in the Central West grain belt of New South Wales, Australia. *(Courtesy Pioneer Park Museum, Parkes, Australia)*

The remarkable Saunderson Type A

An event of major importance occurred in mid-2002, when Newton Williams completed his six-year restoration of a 1908 Saunderson Type A, one of only two remaining in the world. This British tractor ranks in historical significance with the sole surviving examples of the 1911 Wallis Bear, the 1915 Ewing Ford B and the 1916 John Deere Dain. These tractors are world heritage treasures, owing to their uniqueness and the documented evidence of incidents that occurred during their early days.

In 1907 a report was tabled to the South Australian State Parliament by Mr WP Cummins, MP, stating that draught horses had increased in value almost threefold during the previous ten years. Their upkeep had also apparently risen exorbitantly. He suggested that consideration be given by the Minister of Agriculture, The Honorable L O'Loughlin, to investigate the feasibility of the government purchasing a British-made 'agricultural motor' for the purpose of comparing its cost and ability to that of a team of horses.

The matter was placed before Mr Arthur J Perkins, principal of the government-owned Roseworthy Agricultural College, who advised the minister that the purchase should proceed. Payment was duly allocated for the shipping and purchase of one of Messrs HP Saunderson & Company's 50 brake hp Universal Agricultural Motors, plus matching plough, to be transported from England to Roseworthy Agricultural College.

The Saunderson had been selected on account of the impressive medals it had been awarded in 'Africa, America and various European states'. Mr Perkins considered the company had excellent credentials in agricultural motors, as it had been manufacturing them since 1897 (interestingly this refutes the theory that Dan Albone's Ivel of 1903 was Britain's first lightweight tractor). As a consequence, Perkins considered the Saunderson the most suitable tractor for the purpose of conducting the necessary tests to determine the appropriateness of an agricultural motor replacing a horse team on economic grounds.

With considerable expectation, the 3-wheeled Saunderson arrived at Roseworthy College in July 1908 and was placed in the care of Mr JL Williams, the college's farm mechanic. The tractor was immediately put to work in a variety of jobs and precise records of its performance and costs were documented.

That particular year turned out to be hot and dry in South Australia. It was quickly discovered that the Saunderson 4-furrow plough, which had been delivered with the tractor, was incapable of penetrating the sun-baked soil. It had obviously been designed for the deep ploughing, soft tilth conditions of England. A 3-furrow horse plough was therefore modified and hitched to the drawbar of the tractor by a chain.

It also became obvious that the tractor cooling system appeared to be inadequate for the torrid summer conditions. Frequent stops had to be made to drain the boiling water from the radiator and refill it with cold water. (Most readers will be appalled by this action of draining the boiling water and refilling immediately with cold water. Such an action indicates a lack of understanding of the physics relating to the rapid expansion and contraction of metals and the disastrous effect it could, and did, have on the water jacketing of the Saunderson engine.)

A person having only a slight knowledge of early tractors could not fail to be impressed, if not amazed, by the advanced technical design concept of the 1908 Saunderson. Its 3 all-wheel drive configuration was re-introduced by the makers of the Glasgow in 1919, but with less engineering sophistication than the Saunderson. John Deere had trialled a 3 all-wheel drive in 1916 with the Dain tractor, but its design was overly complicated and expensive to manufacture. The Saunderson system worked efficiently and rendered the tractor almost bog-proof!

Despite the excellence of the Saunderson's overall design, the records kept by Williams, the mechanic at Roseworthy Agricultural College, show that it in fact developed a number of serious problems. Williams listed the following:

- water pump failure
- radiator fan 'fell to pieces'
- water circulation inadequate
- valve lift cam 'broke into pieces'
- weak valve springs
- valves 'collapsed'
- fuel pipes cracked
- fuel tank 'shook to pieces'
- gudgeon pins required re-manufacturing
- gear components 'bending and breaking'.

Master restorer Newton Williams (no relation to JL) is emphatic when he states that the failures of the Roseworthy Saunderson were almost entirely due to the lack of JL Williams' mechanical knowledge and his failure to initiate a program of preventative maintenance. During the extensive restoration program, Newton Williams discovered ample evidence to back up his theory and insists the tractor was a well-engineered unit and in the right hands would have performed quite satisfactorily. The results of British and European tests, plus an abundance of surviving testimonials, support his views.

Regardless, a far-reaching and sombre report was read out to the South Australian Parliament on 12 August 1909, by the Honorable Minister for

Specifications of Saunderson Type A

Manufacturer: Saunderson
Country of origin: England
Engine make: Saunderson Elstow
Type: 4-cyl. F head (one overhead inlet valve and one side exhaust valve per cylinder)
Fuel: petrol–kerosene
Cooling: water, forced circulation, radiator
Hp: 50 brake
Rpm: governed 900
Bore and stroke: 6 x 6in (referred to as square)
Ignition: battery high tension trembler coil start–magneto run
Spark plugs: two per cylinder
Spark advance: mechanical–coupled to throttle
Carburettor: float feed
Drive: all three wheels–on suspension
Gears: fully enclosed–2.5, 3.5, 7.5mph–forward and reverse (shuttle)
Steering: Ackerman
Drawbar pull: 18 tons at 7mph on hard level surface
Tipping lorry body: capacity 2 tons
Wheels: 3½ft diameter and 8in width
Weight: 3.5 tons

This rare 1908 photo shows students at the Roseworthy Agricultural College gaining 'agricultural motor experience' with the Saunderson Type A. The attached plough is not the Saunderson-designed 4-furrow plough supplied with the tractor, as it proved unable to penetrate the sun-baked Australian paddocks. The plough pictured is a modified 3-furrow horse plough. *(Courtesy Don Beaty)*

Agriculture, for the year ending 30 June. In essence, the report was scathing of the Saunderson tractor. It concluded, '… we can however only state that the tractor as we have found it is not an implement, the purchase of which, can in any way be recommended to farmers [as a replacement for the horse].'

Such a negative ministerial proclamation had a rippling effect throughout the entire farming community. Despite the sterling efforts of Australian tractor designers AH McDonald and brothers Norman and Felix Caldwell, plus the arrival in the country of both Ivel and International tractors, the progress of farm mechanisation throughout the nation became protracted as a consequence of this parliamentary statement. The irony of the situation is clear when it is considered that the Minister's report was the direct result of a farm mechanic who had failed to grasp the rapidly expanding engineering concepts of the time!

If blame is to be attributed, it should first be with HP Saunderson & Company for not having the foresight to arrange for an engineer to accompany their first tractor to Australia, considering the potential follow-up sales. Secondly, the South Australian Government should have accepted responsibility for not insisting that this occur and for not engaging a farm mechanic who was thoroughly conversant with the new technology.

What is important today, however, is that the Saunderson has somehow miraculously survived and, thanks to the expertise of Newton Williams and his team, who undertook what must have been a most daunting restoration, this extraordinarily important historic icon has been preserved for posterity. It may be inspected at the Pioneer Settlement in Swan Hill, Australia. The only other remaining example in the world is in the caring hands of the folks at the Western Development Museum in Saskatoon, Canada.

The Saunderson Elstow 4-cylinder engine had an advanced ignition system with two spark plugs per cylinder. It also featured overhead inlet and side exhaust valves, which were re-introduced half a century later by Land Rover. A 4-cylinder engine in a 1908 tractor is worthy of contemplation! *(Courtesy G Williams)*

The following description of the Saunderson Type A is taken verbatim from a 1907 Saunderson brochure:

Our now famous three wheel tractor is spring mounted on steel travelling wheels, all of which propel. It is steered by two front wheels, and the third or back wheel is driven from the balance gear of the differential shaft. It will be seen from this that neither of the two front wheels can slip unless the rear wheel slips also, yet when rounding a corner, owing to the track of the rear wheel being midway between the other two, the differential action is unfettered. This feature gives this motor the greatest hauling power it is possible to obtain, as the entire weight rests on the propelling wheels, and no one wheel can slip by itself—the fundamental point of agricultural traction being grip of the ground, beyond which no amount of power would avail, and great weight is not permissible on the land. It is adapted for threshing, ploughing (up to 6 furrows), binding, mowing, hauling, etc.

A front view of the restored ex-Roseworthy 1908 Saunderson Type A. The unit is the jewel in the collection of vintage tractors at the Pioneer Settlement, Swan Hill, Australia. Following nearly a century of abandonment and neglect, it now starts and runs like brand new. *(Courtesy N Williams)*

The rear view of the Saunderson shows the drive to the rear wheel, the lorry box and the passenger seat. *(Courtesy N Williams)*

Opposite page, top: The 3 all-wheel drive John Deere Dain tractor, produced from 1916 to 1919, was powered by a 4-cylinder 24 belt hp engine. It featured an unusual but complicated 2-speed transmission which could be changed on the move under full power. Drive to the three wheels was by roller chain. The Dain proved overly expensive to manufacture and its reliability was compromised by mechanical problems. The company decided to concentrate on its proven and well-accepted Waterloo Boy range of tractors. *(Courtesy Deere & Co., Moline)*

THE 3-WHEEL DRIVE PRINCIPLE

There are three persuasive arguments to commend the concept of the Saunderson 3-wheel drive configuration for farm tractors. These were understood also by Deere and Company of Moline, USA and John Wallace and Sons of Scotland. They are as follows:

- No individual wheel follows in another's track, thus reducing compaction pressures and in soft conditions rendering the tractor less likely to bog.
- Traction is substantially increased compared to conventional 2-wheel drive.
- The drive train is less intricate than 4-wheel drive.

The 3 all-wheel drive Glasgow was the brain-child of William Guthrie and was produced in a disused munitions factory at Cardonald, near Glasgow, Scotland, from 1919 until 1924. The front-drive axle was unique in not incorporating a differential. Instead, each wheel hub was fitted with a pawl and ratchet drive, permitting smooth turning by allowing the outside wheel to speed up whilst the other continued at the sustained speed in relation to the rear wheel. Interestingly though, in reverse gear the ratchets disen-gaged the front-wheel drive so the Glasgow became a single-wheel drive. At the Lincoln tractor trials in 1919, a Glasgow recorded the highest pull-to-weight ratio of any tractor. The example pictured is on display at the Pioneer Settlement, Swan Hill, Australia. *(Courtesy M Daw)*

The Rumely Oil Pull classics

In 1909 the M Rumely Company of La Porte, Indiana, USA, released for public comment a giant experimental tractor. Its twin cylinder engine was designed specifically to run on kerosene. The factory team responsible for its assembly appropriately christened the big tractor 'Kerosene Annie'. Kerosene Annie was vigorously tested and improvements implemented. Around twelve months later Rumely released its first production model, known as the Rumely Oil Pull 25-40 Model B. But the tractors that firmly established Rumely as a major player in the US tractor scene were the two models that followed the B: the Rumely Oil Pull 30-66 Model E and the Rumely Oil Pull 15-30 Model F.

Of all the eighteen Oil Pull models produced from 1910 until the company was taken over by the Allis Chalmers Corporation in 1931, the models E and F were the most outstanding. This should not be construed as indicating the other models were in any way deficient in performance or engineering integrity. However, when considered within the parameters of the very beginning of the tractor evolution, a time when each new design constituted a voyage into the unknown, both the E and F joined an elite group of mechanical contraptions that were capable of performing the required tasks continually, reliably, efficiently and without incurring undue stresses or wear.

The term 'Oil Pull' was coined to highlight the fact that Rumely engines were custom-built to be fuelled with kerosene. This was in the era when internal combustion engines were normally fuelled with the more highly refined and expensive petrol.

Some engine designers had developed a hot box system in the manifold, enabling a petrol engine to be switched over to kerosene fuel following a warm-up period. With the Rumely, a patented Higgins carburettor was used exclusively. This ingenious device enabled the Oil Pull to be started with only a brief 'snort' of petrol. The carburettor was controlled by an advanced design, oil-immersed governor which enabled an instantly variable measure of kerosene and water to be drawn into the combustion chamber. The accepted irregular running of an early kerosene-fuelled tractor was not evident in a Rumely, owing to the highly responsive Higgins carburettor, with its immediate sensitivity to the slightest load variation, signalled by the governor.

The automatic metering of water as fuel into the combustion chamber, although not exclusive to Rumely, was a more scientific process than the system in other engines. The Higgins carburettor, which had no floats or springs, under a light load shut off the supply of water to the mixture of kerosene and air. As the engine load increased, a controlled amount of water was progressively introduced into the manifold. The water caused the mixture to detonate more slowly. When the detonation occurred, the water portion became super-heated and returned to its natural elements of hydrogen and oxygen. These elements attached themselves to any free-flying carbon particles, creating a de-coking effect within the cylinder.

The other feature normally associated with the term Oil Pull was the oil-cooling system used by Rumely, as opposed to the common practice of using water as an engine coolant. The utilisation of oil had several advantages, not the least of which was the engine's ability to operate at around 132°C (270°F)—well over the boiling point of water. This high operational temperature permitted an efficiency in the combustion of kerosene fuel that no water-cooled engine could hope to match.

The cooling radiator comprised a number of fabricated galvanised steel sections or tanks. The coolant oil was circulated through the sections from the cylinder jackets by a chain-driven pump. Hot exhaust gases were directed out through the top of the cooling tower. This created an up-draught of cool air around the radiator sections, being drawn in from the bottom of the tower.

A 1911 photo of a Rumely Oil Pull Model E pulling an 8-furrow mouldboard plough. The ploughman's job was hazardous. As seen here, he was obliged to ride his plough balanced on a wooden walkway. Upon arriving at each headland he had to raise, then lower, each individual mouldboard; considerable physical effort was required. A fall in front of the plough usually proved fatal.

The Rumely Oil Pull 15-30 Model F was the baby of the series in 1911. Its chain windlass steering was vague and required constant correction by the operator—a physically demanding job. Consequently, the Dreadnought Guide Self Steer attachment proved a popular optional extra. This was located 13ft ahead of the tractor and included a guide wheel which hugged the land side of the previous furrow. Owned by Bob Bone.

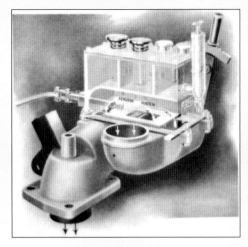

The ingenious Higgins carburettor (used in the Rumely Models E and F) operated without floats, springs or internal self-adjustments. Instead, a slide was automatically controlled by the governor which instantly metered the mixture of kerosene and water to suit the varying work load.

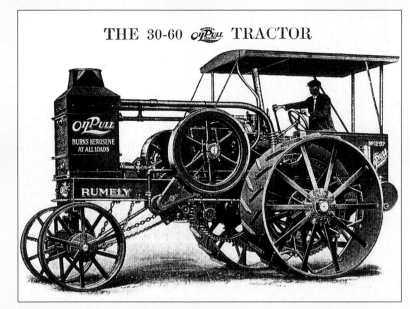

Introduced in 1910, the Model E was Rumely's second production model. It was a truly gigantic tractor with a massive 2-cylinder engine featuring a 10 x 12in bore and stroke. Only one forward and one reverse gear were provided. Common to tractors of the period, the E had totally exposed transmission gears and windlass chain steering, a carry-over from the Rumely steam traction engines. It remained in production until 1923. Over 3000 units were manufactured.

SPECIFICATIONS OF 30-60 OilPull

HORSEPOWER
Tractive. 30
Brake. 60
R. p. m. 375

CYLINDERS
Number. 2
Diameter. . . . . 10 in.
Stroke. . . . . 12 in.

FRAME
Size of I-Beam. . . . . 12 in.
Weight in lbs. per foot. . . 31½ in.

WHEELS
                          Tire Height
Front. . . . . 16 in. 44 in.
Extension (extra). . . . 6 in. 44 in.
Rear. . . . . 30 in. 80 in.
Extension Rim. . . . . . 10 in. 80 in.

SPOKES
Inches Wide. 2¾
Inches Thick. . . . . ¾

DIAMETER OF SHAFTS
Differential. . . . . 4⁷⁄₁₆ in.
Reverse. . . . . 4⅜ in.
Idler. . . . . 3⁵⁄₁₆ in.
Crank Shaft. . . . . 4⁷⁄₁₆ in.

DIAMETER OF AXLES
Front Axle. . . . . 3¼ in.
Rear Axle. . . . . 5⁷⁄₁₆ in.

GEARING
                                      Face   No. of Teeth
Master Gear. . . . . 6 in. 71
Master Pinion. . . . . . . 6¾ in. 11
Second Motion Gear. . . . 4 in. 66
Reversing Gear. . . . . . . 5 in. 25
Small Idler Gear. . . . . . 5 in. 12
Large Idler Gear. . . . . . 5 in. 17
Differential. . . . . 5 in. 63

FLY WHEEL
Diameter. . . . . 48 in.
Weight. . . . . 1300 lb

BAND WHEEL
Face. . . . . 11 in.
Diameter. . . . . 36 in.

SHIPPING WEIGHT IN POUNDS 26,500

GENERAL DIMENSIONS
Extreme Length. . . . . . 19 ft. 0 in.
Extreme Width. . . . . . . 9 ft. 8 in.
Extreme Height. . . . . . 11 ft. 0 in.

LARGE FLY WHEEL GIVES ENGINE STEADY MOTION

FORCED FEED OILER
SPLASH LUBRICATION SYSTEM ALSO USED

PLUNGER FUEL PUMP
FOR KEROSENE AND WATER

EVERY PART ACCESSIBLE FROM PLATFORM

GOVERNOR POSITIVELY CONTROLS SPEED AT ALL LOADS

AIR INLET

SECOR-HIGGINS CARBURETER

FRAME STRONGLY RIVETED

FRAME 9" X 21 POUND I BEAMS

GASOLINE TANK FOR STARTING

MAIN FUEL TANK CARRIES A DAYS SUPPLY

STRONG FLAT SPOKES

CENTRIFUGAL PUMP FOR COOLING SYSTEM

SIDE SLIPPING IMPOSSIBLE

LARGE HIGH DRIVERS 24" FACE 70" HIGH

WHEELS BORED FOR MUD LUGS

No 6894

SPECIFICATIONS OF 15-30 Oil Pull

HORSEPOWER

Tractive 15
Brake 30
R. p. m. 375

CYLINDERS

Number 1
Diameter . . . . 10 in.
Stroke . . . . 12 in.

FRAME

Size of I-Beam . . . . 9 in.
Weight in lbs. per foot 21

WHEELS

	Tire	Height
Front	12 in.	38 in.
Extensions (extra)	6 in.	38 in.
Rear	24 in.	70 in.
Extension Rims	10 in.	70 in.

GEARING

	Face	No. of Teeth
Master Gear	4 in.	73
Master Pinion	$4\frac{1}{2}$ in.	14
Second Motion Gear . .	$3\frac{1}{2}$ in.	90
Reversing Gear	3 in.	22
Small Idler Gear	3 in.	12
Large Idler Gear	3 in.	18
Differential	3 in.	57
Large Differential . . .	3 in.	62
High Speed Gear	3 in.	27

SPOKES

Inches Wide 2
Inches Thick . . . . $\frac{1}{2}$

DIAMETER OF AXLES

Front Axle . . . . $2\frac{1}{2}$ in.
Rear Axle . . . . $4\frac{3}{16}$ in.

DIAMETER OF SHAFTS

Differential . . . . $3\frac{7}{16}$ in.
Reverse . . . . $3\frac{1}{32}$ in.
Idler . . . . $2\frac{7}{8}$ in.
Crank Shaft . . . . $4\frac{7}{16}$ in.

FLY WHEEL

Diameter . . . . $55\frac{1}{4}$ in.
Weight . . . . .1000 lb

BAND WHEEL

Face . . . . $9\frac{1}{2}$ in.
Diameter . . . . 30 in.

SHIPPING WEIGHT IN

POUNDS 16,500

GENERAL DIMENSIONS

Extreme Length . . .16 ft. 0 in.
Extreme Width . . . . . 7 ft. 10 in.
Extreme Height . . . .10 ft. $3\frac{1}{2}$ in.

The Rumely F was unique in being the only Oil Pull to feature a single-cylinder engine. All the other models had two cylinders. It was produced from 1911 to 1918, by which time 3854 had been built. In 1918 the F was uprated from 15-30 to 18-35.

The Moline Universal

It is almost beyond credence that in 1919 there existed a farm tractor equipped with an electric starter motor plus (amazingly) an electric governor! It was even fitted with electric lights, at a time when few homesteads could boast such a luxury. The tractor was the Moline Universal made in the USA at Moline, Illinois.

The origins of the Moline Universal extend back to 1914 when the Universal Tractor Manufacturing Company of Columbus, Ohio, unveiled an oddball front-wheel drive motor cultivator. The spindly tractor was powered by a 10hp, 2-cylinder Reliable engine mounted over the front axle, thus providing weight and traction to the drive wheels.

In 1915 the Universal Tractor Company was purchased by the Moline Plow Company. The new owners persevered with the lightweight tractor until 1918, when the company came under the control of the respected motor designer and entrepreneur John Willys. An all-new 4-cylinder, ohv pressure lubricated engine of 18 belt hp was created and fitted to the re-engineered tractor. The updated machine was designated the Moline Universal Model D.

The new tractor's engine was an advanced design of 3.5 x 5in bore and stroke and had a relatively high 1800rpm. But what placed the Moline Universal at the forefront of tractor engine technology was its optional Remy custom-built electrical system.

At the heart of the system was a 6-volt battery cradled in a softly sprung battery box, gently riding on diminutive leaf springs. Presumably a battery in 1915 was not overly robust and had to be protected from the jolting of a steel-wheeled tractor. The battery supplied energy to a distributor (at a time when magnetos were commonly fitted to tractors) and also to a truly ingenious electric governor.

The controls for the ignition, generator and carburettor were grouped into the one housing located at the right front of the engine block. In front of the operator was a master electric switch gear which operated the lights, ignition and electric governor system. The tractor had only one forward and one reverse gear, but the governor rheostat could be set to one of ten selected engine speeds, thus providing an effective ground working speed of 0.5 to 3.5mph in ten increments.

The engine carburettor was remarkable in having no less than three bowls. The upper bowl received the petrol by gravity feed and had a conventional float. The centre bowl was charged with kerosene, a small quantity of which dripped into the lower bowl. A wick was ignited by a glow plug which in turn was heated by a spark directed from the eight lobe cam of the distributor. Every second impulse sent a spark to the glow plug. The heated kerosene was drawn up into the inlet manifold. It is fascinating to consider that a tiny flame burned constantly within the carburettor whenever the engine was running.

Operating the Model D required a considerable degree of expertise and caution. A concrete counterweight was built into the right-hand driving wheel to compensate for the offset positioning of the engine. Nevertheless it was not difficult to drive the tractor into a compromising situation which could result in a capsize. It was suicidal to attempt to tow-start the engine, as the rear of the tractor would buck into the near-vertical as soon as the clutch was engaged, due to the normal torque reaction on the driving axle being reversed and reacting instantly on the light rear end.

It is not known how many Moline Model D tractors were sold, but the figure is certainly in the thousands, including large numbers being exported around the world. Production was terminated in 1922, by which time the popularity of the motor cultivator type of tractors was in decline.

This advertisement appeared in North American farming periodicals in 1916, by which time the Universal Tractor Manufacturing Company had been acquired by the Moline Plow Company. The line drawing is of the original Moline, powered by the 2-cylinder Reliable engine.

A TRACTOR TALE

Whilst carrying out research in Ohio, USA, in 1997 I spent time with Dan Ehlerding of Jamestown, a noted farmer and classic tractor collector. Dan recounted the time back in 1915 when his grandfather, Howard Ehlerding, traded in his horse team as part-payment against the purchase of a brand new Universal 10hp tractor (motor cultivator). The Universal was duly delivered to the farm on the back of a wagon and unloaded.

With great expectations and anticipation, Mr Ehlerding watched as the agent proceeded to go through the motions of starting the engine. This proved to be a dismal anticlimax, as the engine simply refused to start. Over the following week the agent returned daily to the farm armed with an assortment of tools, but failed to start the Reliable 2-cylinder engine; it appeared the engine was reliable in name only.

A factory Universal technician was eventually summoned from the plant at nearby Columbus. The week grew into a month and still the engine declined to start. In desperation, an engineer from the Reliable Engine Company headquarters at Portsmouth, Ohio, was called in to solve the problem. (It is interesting to contemplate the obvious laid-back attitude, compared with how such a serious matter would be treated today. But of course all this occurred in 1915.) Parts were exchanged, components were dismantled and inspected, but inexplicably the engine still could not be fired into life.

Mr Ehlerding was a patient man but the situation was by now desperate. There were acres waiting to be tilled and the trade-in horse team had already been sold by the agent. A thoroughly frustrated and disillusioned Mr Ehlerding decided to have no further dealings with the tractor agent. It had taken a lot of persuasion for him to even consider one of these 'new fangled' tractors and now he regretted that decision. There was only one thing left to do. He contacted a reputable horse trader and negotiated a deal whereby he purchased a complete horse team—and traded in his tractor!

Is it possible this was the only occasion in history when a tractor was traded against the purchase of a team of horses?

A truly outstanding example of a 1919 Moline Universal D. Owner Mal Cameron completely dismantled and overhauled what was originally a disaster with a seized engine. The unit is now complete, including all the electrics, which makes it special; the majority of remaining examples are minus their electrics or were never fitted with them. Note the convenient position of the belt pulley, however it was directly coupled to the engine and could not be disengaged whilst the engine was running.

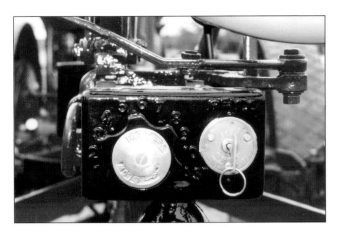

Above left: This control box was positioned immediately in front of the operator. The left-hand control adjusted the electric governor and thus the engine rpm. The right-hand switch was for the ignition and lights. It is likely that this was the first model of tractor to have the security of an ignition switch key.

Above right: Pictured is the 3-bowl carburettor and the black box enclosing the generator plus controls for the carburettor and ignition. The dial at the left of the picture indicates oil pressure and the gauge at the right, below the carburettor, is a sump oil level indicator. The glass pre-filter bowl is the original, fitted to the tractor in 1919.

Left: This view of the Moline Universal Model D shows the offset position of the engine, which provided the operator with an uninterrupted view of the plough furrow. Note also the high clearance under the tractor, which made it suitable for row crop work. However, it lacked the advantages of variable wheel widths, a feature of the later designated row crop tractors.

The industrial cousins

By the end of the first decade of the 20th century, the main thrust of the tractor evolution was taking place in North America. Australian, British and European tractors were emerging but, understandably perhaps, in much lesser numbers. By 1910, fifteen manufacturers in the USA had produced around 4000 tractors—this represented double the previous year's output. But considering that the farm horse and mule population of that year was close to 25 000 000 animals, to see a tractor working on an American farm at that time was still a very rare experience. Accordingly, on the occasion when a tractor was observed clattering its way around a field, it was common for a curious crowd of spectators to gather and stare in fascination.

Among those keen to observe the new tractors were quarry masters, road building engineers, lumber contractors and others who traditionally used animals or steam power to haul payloads. They quickly realised that a farm tractor, perhaps with certain modifications, would perform their industrial tasks with a greater degree of economy and speed.

Tractor producers were quick to encourage this unexpected interest in their products and welcomed the additional orders originating from non-farm users. They listened to suggestions from this new group of customers and displayed a keenness to introduce modifications which made the farm tractor more appropriate for industrial applications. Responding to the trend, it was not long before special factory-designed industrial models were included in tractor catalogues.

The tractor which proved most popular with urban and county authorities for industrial applications was the Fordson Model F. Introduced in 1917 against an order from the British Government for 6000 units, it became the world's top seller during the 1920s. Approximately 750 000 were distributed around the world. The Model F was an unsophisticated machine, rough to drive but priced well below any of its competitors. Opposition American tractor companies either lowered their prices to compete or went out of business.

By the end of the 1920s it was not uncommon for tractors pulling road graders to be encountered along country roads. Others were equipped with buffers and used in railway shunting yards and tram depots. A variety of cranes were mounted, trailed or pushed, with winches operated by belt pulleys or later by power-take-off shafts. Solid rubber tyres were fitted to special wheels, as distinct from the steel-lugged wheels used in farming; this enabled these industrialised tractors to travel on paved roads. Higher gearing was provided, as the tractors with rubber tyres could travel faster than their steel-wheeled counterparts, which were limited to around 5mph. In Europe in the late 1920s, pneumatic tyres became available for tractors and in 1932 Allis Chalmers introduced the concept to North America.

Bulldozer blades became popular attachments for crawler tractors in the 1930s. Front-end and over-loaders followed in the late 1930s, then became commonplace after World War II.

In the 1950s, hydraulic power technology came of age, replacing cable winches for the operation of bulldozer blades and accelerating the development of sophisticated front-end loaders and cranes. Torque converters and power shift transmissions replaced the manual transmissions when industrialised farm tractors were used for earth-moving and construction applications. Also, hydraulically operated shuttle directional clutches were introduced. Power steering became the accepted norm for all industrial tractors. A front-end loader equipped with a torque converter, power shift transmission, shuttle directional

The Australian-designed and built 1912 Caldwell Vale, which was a transport version of the Caldwell Vale 80hp agricultural tractor. Remarkably, both the tractor and transporter featured 4-wheel drive, 4-wheel brakes and 4-wheel power steering. The 4-cylinder, 680cu in, petrol–kerosene-fuelled motor had a 6.5in bore and stroke, and developed 80bhp at 800rpm. A Bosch magneto and trembler coil supplied the electrical impulse to the two spark plugs per cylinder. A three forward and one reverse speed gearbox was fully enclosed. Restored by Reg Schuster.

control and hydraulic power steering could drastically reduce the cycle time of loading a truck or hopper, when compared to a loader on a conventional farm tractor.

With the arrival of the 1960s, the modified farm tractor had been replaced with purpose-built industrial and construction tractors. Today, the non-farm tasks allocated to straight, unmodified agricultural tractors are restricted to light work such as kerb mowing, road broom operation, park and recreational area maintenance and golf course applications.

The Four-Drive Tractor Company of Michigan, USA, introduced a new model 4-wheel drive tractor in 1920, known as the Fitch Four-Drive Model D4. Its Climax 4-cylinder engine developed 35bhp at 800rpm. A number were equipped with solid rubber tyres and sold with a centre-mounted grader blade designed for road maintenance. This ultra-rare example is a feature of the Gunnedah Rural Museum, Australia. The operator is Graham Cameron.

Right & middle: These two photos, taken eighty-two years apart at the same location, are of the same tractor, pulling the same boring plant and stationary engine. The tractor is a 1912 International Mogul Type C powered by a Famous single-cylinder 20hp engine. Purchased new by the Daniels family, it was the first-ever tractor delivered to the Queensland Central Highlands in Australia. Following two seasons of ploughing, the Mogul was relegated to the status of an industrial tractor and used solely for hauling the Southern Cross No. 2 boring plant (used for sinking artesian bores). In 1917 the tractor's engine disintegrated and the unit was abandoned. The first photo was taken in 1916 and the second in 1998, following a mammoth restoration by Andy Plunkett and a large team of volunteers. The tractor is now back in the care of the Daniels family. *(Courtesy A Plunkett)*

Below: This 1913 photo shows two Holt Caterpillar tractors involved in haulage work in Nevada, USA. Note the tricycle steering. The engine was a 4-cylinder unit designed to run on petrol–kerosene. The photo was taken by Joshua M Pawley, a Welsh-born executive engineer for Holt Manufacturing Company in California. He was posted to Australia in 1913 as the country's manager for the company. *(Courtesy David Bell)*

A composite picture featured in the March 1999 edition of the *Fordson Times*. It clearly indicates the versatility of the tractor and the ingenuity of industrial equipment designers of the period. It is interesting to contemplate the reaction from today's government safety officers if required to approve some of the attachments. *(Courtesy Mal Brinkmann)*

It is difficult to identify the Case 12-20 Crossmount tractor buried under this 1927 New Zealand-made Boothmac grader. The complexity of the controls suggests the operator would have required strong muscles and a quick response! Owned by Noel Sheat.

Allis Chalmers produced an extensive range of fine motor graders commencing in 1932. In 1940 the lightweight Patrol grader was introduced, built around the WC farm tractor. There were no hydraulics and the blade was raised and lowered manually. Owned by Barry Hughes.

This British-designed 1940s Fowler crane is mounted upon an International WD6 farm tractor. Operator vision was dangerously restricted and, adding to the problem, the articulated crane steered in the opposite direction to the turning of the steering wheel. Roy Ford's Fowler is a reminder of the hazards that could be involved in operating early construction machinery.

Pat O'Brien still uses this 1940s British Chaseside Loader on his farm in Queensland, Australia. The cable is driven by a winch mounted on the rear pto shaft. The unwieldy contraption is mounted on a Fordson E27N tractor powered by a Perkins P6 diesel engine.

British Standard Machinery Company custom-built this hydraulically operated Britstand bulldozer to fit the German Hanomag K55 crawler tractor in 1950. Note the short-stroke hydraulic cylinders and the exposed high-pressure hoses located immediately in front of the operator's face. Regardless, Britstand dozer attachments earned an excellent reputation for reliability and in-built structural strength.
(Britstand promotional material)

Massey Ferguson released its British-built Workbull in 1960. It was based on the agricultural MF 35 and powered by a Standard 23C 4-cylinder diesel engine of 37.35 brake hp (earlier Workbulls were produced in the USA). The majority were sold with the MF 710 backhoe and the MF 702 front-end loader. The tractor name was soon changed from Workbull to 203 and powered by a Perkins diesel 3/152 3-cylinder engine. The Workbull pictured had a Sears rotary mower attached to its 3-point linkage. The driver is Gib Gospal.

Beneath the handsome styling of the 1963 Whitlock 66 Loader is a Fordson Super Major equipped with a heavy duty industrial front axle, clutch and rear axle housings. Whitlock earthmovers were made by Whitlock Bros Ltd of Great Yeldham, England. The operator is Bill Flett.

AS Hydor of Haderslev, Denmark, offered a range of air compressors designed for mounting to a tractor's 3-point linkage and driven by the pto shaft. Pictured is a Hydor A105 which achieved 149cfm at 100psi. The tractor is a Chamberlain Champion.

A Ford 3000 farm tractor was used as the base unit for this Conquip 6-ton mobile crane. This promotional photo of 1966 suggested that the crane was so easy to drive that a housewife could use it to go shopping! The model is Margery Daw.

Showing off the power of its hydraulics, demonstrator Bill O'Connor elevates the JCB 3C loader backhoe on its front and rear hydraulic arms to enable a Morris Mini Moke to be driven underneath the tractor. JCB earthmovers were made at Uttoxeter, Staffordshire, UK.

This photo, taken in Canberra, Australia, around 1962, is of a Whitlock 60-66 loader backhoe turning the first sod of what was to become Lake Burley Griffin. These early Whitlock units used a Fordson Power Major farm tractor as a base. Included in the photo is a Holden utility Lough Equipment service vehicle and a Thwaites Nimbus Diesel Dumper. The original Australian Parliament building is in the background.

From a 1930 Catalogue

MALCOLM MOORE

ELECTRIC WELDING EQUIPMENT

For fitting to the Fordson

The Fordson fitted with Electric Welding Equipment.

Used by Melbourne and Metropolitan Board of Works for jointing pipes be electric welding, and repairing pipe lines and steel structures in the field.

The same type of equipment is available as a Portable Electric Lighting Set.

This picture of a Fordson Model F agricultural tractor fitted with a Malcolm Moore electric welder was taken from the 1930 catalogue for Malcolm Moore & Company. The unit was used for joining pipes by electric welding, and repairing pipe lines and steel structures in the field. A similar rig was also available as a portable electric lighting set. *(Courtesy* Fordson Times*)*

Lightweights

Heavyweight tractors capture the imagination of historians of farm mechanisation. However, the engineering diversity of lightweight tractors is no less dramatic and fascinating. Indeed, the lightweights outnumbered their larger brethren, simply due to the fact that, globally, the percentage of small holdings far exceeded that of broadacre properties, a situation which remains the same today.

Predictably, the greatest number of the lightweights were made in Europe, where scores of manufacturers entered the tractor arena during the first half of the 20th century. Some, such as the German companies Heinrich Lanz in Mannheim and Xaver Fendt in Marktoberdorf, were to become familiar tractor names worldwide. Others, including Linke-Hofmann-Busch in Breslau, Germany, and the Swiss manufacturer Vevey in Montreux, largely confined the distribution of their small production run, purpose-built machines to within their own regions.

North America and Britain produced some excellent lightweights, but seldom with the degree of sophistication of the European machines. However, American classics such as the Allis Chalmers B and International McCormick A were produced in vast numbers and sold to farmers around the world. Harry Ferguson's TE series, manufactured in Coventry, England, and his American TO series, manufactured in Detroit, USA, were undoubtedly among the all-time great tractors.

There were also a few lightweights that could only be described as lacking in design integrity. These inept tractors mainly appeared immediately after World War II, a time during which there was an extreme shortage of tractors. Entrepreneurs, anxious to cash in on the seller's market and usually with little or no previous tractor expertise, rushed untested machines into rural showrooms in the hope of making quick profits. The majority proved to be well below acceptable standards, both in performance and design. Ironically, the few remaining examples of these have become much coveted collector items today.

This chapter examines a small cross-section of lightweight farm tractors from around the world that emerged during the classic era. The term lightweight is applied loosely, without horsepower or weight parameters. The sole criteria for inclusion in this chapter is that farmers would have classified the tractor as lightweight at the time the tractor was in production. The examples selected represent the first six decades of the 20th century.

A line of classic lightweights. Pictured are members of the Harry Ferguson Tractor Club Australasia Inc. lining up at the Lake Goldsmith Rally, Australia.

Allgaier R22

Manufacturer: Allgaier Werkzeughbau
Country of origin: Germany
Period of manufacture: 1949–52
Engine make: own
Fuel: diesel
Cooling: water
Hp: 22 brake
Rpm: 1500
No. of cylinders: 1
Bore and stroke: 125 x 150mm
Cubic capacity: 1840cc
Gears forward: 4
Gears reverse: 1
Drawbar pull: n/a
Weight: 1500kg

Allgaier R22

This ubiquitous German classic was built around the company's outdated but immensely rugged hopper-cooled engine. Despite its primitive appearance, it was a very capable tractor. It reeked of character and is very much a collectable icon today. Owned by Ross Hungerford.

Allis Chambers B

Manufacturer: Allis Chalmers Manufacturing Co.
Country of origin: USA
Period of manufacture: 1937–57
Engine make: own
Fuel: petrol–kerosene
Cooling: water
Hp: 22.25 belt
Rpm: 1500
No. of cylinders: 4
Bore and stroke: 3.375 x 3.5in*
Cubic capacity: 125.3cu in
Gears forward: 3
Gears reverse: 1
Drawbar pull: 2667lbs at 2.42mph
Weight: 2251lbs
3.25in bore until 1942. Also produced in England.

Allis Chambers B

This was one of the most successful lightweights of all time. Credited as being the first American tractor for sale on pneumatic tyres without a steel wheel option. A tricycle version, the model C, was also produced. The Allis Chambers B was thoroughly dependable and easy to drive, but involved a great deal of athleticism to climb up into the seat. Owned by the author.

BMB President

Manufacturer: Brockhouse Engineering Ltd
Country of origin: England
Period of manufacture: 1950–56
Engine make: Morris
Fuel: petrol–kerosene
Cooling: water
Hp: belt 12.6
Rpm: 2500
No. of cylinders: 4
Bore and stroke: 2.244 x 3.543in
Cubic capacity: 59.86cu in
Gears forward: 3
Gears reverse: 1
Drawbar pull: 2050lbs at 1.6mph
Weight: 1875lbs

BMB President

The BMB (British Motor Boat) President looked cute and ran sweetly, but it was an engineering apology in its time. With its dangerous seating and inadequate brakes, hazardous throttle control, poor gear ratios and non-standard 3-point linkage, it was never a threat to the Ferguson! Owned by James Flower.

The advertisement below appeared in numerous Australian rural magazines in 1958. It indicates that there was still unsold stock two years after production had ceased.

Bailor

Manufacturer: Bailor Plow Manufacturing Co.
Country of origin: USA
Period of manufacture: 1921–30
Engine make: LeRoi
Fuel: petrol
Cooling: water
Hp: 12 belt
Rpm: 1200
No. of cylinders: 4
Bore and stroke: 3.165 x 4.25in
Cubic capacity: 142cu in
Gears forward: 2
Gears reverse: 1
Drawbar pull: n/a
Weight: 1990lbs

Bailor

Originally powered by a 2-cylinder Cushman engine, this model featured the more powerful and much heavier 4-cylinder LeRoi. The extra hp caused the flimsy girder frame to flex alarmingly. A farmer operating a Bailor had considerable difficulty seeing ahead, whilst toes and elbows were always at risk of being caught in the drive chains. Vague worm steering added to the problems.

Bristol 20

Manufacturer: Bristol Tractors Ltd
Country of origin: England
Period of manufacture: 1949–56
Engine make: Austin
Fuel: petrol–kerosene
Cooling: water
Hp: 22 Brake
Rpm: 1500
No. of cylinders: 4
Bore and stroke: 3.125 x 4.375in
Cubic capacity: 134cu in
Gears forward: 3
Gears reverse: 1
Drawbar pull: 3750 lbs at 1.85mph
Weight: 3000lbs

Bristol 20

The Bristol 20 was a very capable British crawler with a long pedigree. The Austin engine was the same as that used in the Austin A70 car and provided the Bristol 20 with dynamic performance. A clever carburettor automatically switched fuels from petrol to kerosene. Owned by Catherine Scouller.

Case S-EX

This model was an export-only version of the Model S, originally intended for the Scandinavian market. It was handsomely styled but had old-technology chain final drives and hand clutch. However, these presented no problems and the S-EX was a very capable, basic tractor; it was pleasant to operate and had a good reserve of power. Only 3627 were produced.

Case S-EX

Manufacturer: JI Case Company
Country of origin: USA
Period of manufacture: 1941–53
Engine make: own
Fuel: petrol–kerosene
Cooling: water
Hp: 21.62 brake
Rpm: 1550
No. of cylinders: 4
Bore and stroke: 4 x 3.5in*
Cubic capacity: 154cu in
Gears forward: 4
Gears reverse: 1
Drawbar pull: 3166lbs at 2.29mph
Weight: 4380lbs
Cylinder bore increased in 1953 to 3.625in from serial No. 8027115.

Caterpillar 10

The smallest of the Caterpillar family, these narrow lightweights were used extensively in orchards where they could work within tree rows originally laid out for single horse accommodation. Integrity of design was the reason Caterpillar became the world's largest producer of crawler tractors. Owned by L Kahl.

Caterpillar 10

Manufacturer: Caterpillar Tractor Co.*
Country of origin: USA
Period of manufacture: 1928–33
Engine make: own
Fuel: petrol
Cooling: water
Hp: 18.1 brake
Rpm: 1500
No. of cylinders: 4
Bore and stroke: 3.375 x 4in
Cubic capacity: 143cu in
Gears forward: 3
Gears reverse: 1
Drawbar pull: 2816lbs at 1.98mph
Weight: 4575lbs
Produced three years after CL Best Gas Traction Co. and Holt Manufacturing Co. amalgamated in 1925 to form the Caterpillar Tractor Co.

Eicher EM 200

Manufacturer: Gebr. Eicher Traktoren
Country of origin: Germany*
Period of manufacture: 1959–
Engine make: own
Fuel: diesel
Cooling: air
Hp: 25 brake
Rpm: 2000
No. of cylinders: 2
Bore and stroke: 100 x 125mm
Cubic capacity: 1962cc
Gears forward: 5
Gears reverse: 1
Drawbar pull: n/a
Weight: 1430kg
Also made under licence by Eicher Goodearth Ltd, India.

Eicher EM 200

When the EM 200 was introduced, Eicher had already earned an enviable reputation for producing dependable tractors and had become one of Germany's major tractor producers. In 1959, when the Eicher EM 200 was first produced, there were few finer engineered lightweight tractors than this. It included Bosch-designed live hydraulics. Owner Mal Cameron. *(Courtesy M Blake)*

Eron D

Manufacturer: Soc. An. Meroni. Co.
Country of origin: Italy
Period of manufacture: 1950
Engine make: Condor
Fuel: diesel
Cooling: air
Hp: 12 brake
Rpm: 1850
No. of cylinders: 1
Bore and stroke: 100 x 106mm
Cubic capacity: 832cc
Gears forward: 6
Gears reverse: 2
Drawbar pull: 2866lbs at 2mph
Weight: 900kg

Eron D

A rare Italian masterpiece. With its Pirrelli 750 x 16 tyres, this all-wheel drive could almost climb trees. An outstanding powerhouse in a small package, the Eron D was perfect for the Lombardi farmlands for which it was designed. Remarkably, this example has never worked in its life. Driver Peter Sultana.

Empire 88

A quirky little tractor with a Jeep engine, gearbox and transfer case, which was never tested at Nebraska test facility. The Empire 88 was hair-raising to drive in top gear (22.5mph) but served as a good utility tractor around the farm. An estimated 6800 were produced with 2000 sold into South America.* This tractor enjoys a cult following today. *(Courtesy K Miller)*
*Figures from Empire Owners Club, NY State, but are largely unsubstantiated.

Empire 88

Manufacturer: Empire Tractor Corporation
Country of origin: USA
Period of manufacture: 1946–48
Engine make: Willys Overland
Fuel: petrol
Cooling: water
Hp: 40 brake
Rpm: 2000
No. of cylinders: 4
Bore and stroke: 3.175 x 4.375in
Cubic capacity: 134.6cu in
Gears forward: 6
Gears reverse: 2
Drawbar pull: n/a
Weight: 2450lbs

Ferguson TED

The Ferguson TE, in Britain, and TO, in the USA, revolutionised mechanised agriculture, on account of Harry Ferguson's patented Ferguson System of linkage and hydraulics, plus the comprehensive range of 35 custom-designed implements which the tractor could operate. It is now considered one of the all-time great tractors. Owned by H and G Shaw. *(Courtesy H Shaw)*

Ferguson TED

The figures below relate to the TED model. Figures for the TEA (petrol) and TEF (diesel) would differ.

Manufacturer: Standard Cars Ltd
Country of origin: England
Period of manufacture: 1949–56 (TE series introduced 1946)
Engine make: Standard (Continental in early petrol models)
Fuel: petrol–kerosene
Cooling: water
Hp: 26.1 belt
Rpm: 2000
No. of cylinders: 4
Bore and stroke: 85 x 92mm (bore increased from 80mm to 85mm in 1951)
Cubic capacity: 127.4cu in
Gears forward: 4
Gears reverse: 1
Drawbar pull: 2800lbs at 2.66mph
Weight: 2500lbs

Ferguson promotional material contributed considerably to the universal acceptance of the Ferguson System of mechanised farming. This is an example of one of many differing advertisements which appeared in 1951 British farming magazines and, in this instance, highlighted the ease and conve-nience of owning a Ferguson tractor with an attached Ferguson 3-point linkage, rear-mounted sickle mower.

CUT **WORKING COSTS** AS WELL AS **GRASS**

WITH THE FERGUSON TRACTOR-MOUNTED MOWER

You'll have easier, swifter mowing, with fewer delays than ever before with the Ferguson Mower. Tractor-mounted, power operated, it cuts a 5 ft. swathe at speeds up to 3¼ m.p.h. in second gear under all conditions.

The knife speed of the Ferguson mower is considerably above average, and thus deals more efficiently with the short type of grass cut for silage and grass drying. A break-away mechanism in the pull bar protects the cutter bar from damage on hitting obstacles, and avoids costly delays on uneven ground. The cutter bar is located just behind the tractor rear wheels, and this, combined with the use of the hydraulic lift and independent rear wheel brakes gives the quickest turns and highest degree of manoeuvrability you've ever found on a mower.

The mower can be attached and detached from the tractor by one man in a matter of minutes. It's one of the finest Ferguson aids to more efficient, more economical farming.

Ask your local Ferguson Dealer for a free demonstration on your farm and about the Ferguson Pay-as-you-Farm Plan.

ON ANY SIZE FARM — IT WILL PAY YOU, TOO — TO

FARM WITH FERGUSON

Ferguson tractors are manufactured for Harry Ferguson Ltd., Coventry, by The Standard Motor Company Limited

Ford 9N

Manufacturer: Ford Motor Co.
Country of origin: USA
Period of manufacture: 1939–42*
Engine make: own
Fuel: petrol
Cooling: water
Hp: 23.83 belt
Rpm: 2000
No. of cylinders: 4
Bore and stroke: 3.187 x 3.75in
Cubic capacity: 120cu in
Gears forward: 3
Gears reverse: 1
Drawbar pull: 2236lbs at 2.11mph
Weight: 2340lbs
A wartime utility version, the 2N, was produced from 1942 until 1947, when it was replaced by the 8N.

Ford 9N

The lightweight Ford 9N regained for Ford the status it previously had (and lost) of being one of the USA's major tractor companies. Apart from the Ferguson type A, it was the first tractor to go into mass production incorporating the Ferguson System of hydraulically controlled 3-point linkage implement hitch. The Ford 9N had a similar profile to the later Ferguson TE and TO series but was a totally different tractor. Owned by Mal Cameron. *(Courtesy M Blake)*

Guldner AF 30

Manufacturer: Guldner Motoren Werke
Country of origin: Germany
Period of manufacture: 1948–53
Engine make: own
Fuel: diesel
Cooling: water
Hp: 30 brake
Rpm: 1800
No. of cylinders: 2
Bore and stroke: 105 x 150mm
Cubic capacity: 2600cc
Gears forward: 5
Gears reverse: 1
Drawbar pull: n/a
Weight: 1960kg

Guldner AF 30

Outdated even in 1949, only a year after it was first made, but indestructible! The Guldner AF 30 was typical of the high standard of indigenous engineering of most German tractors. This unit was powered with Guldner's own engine, but a number of AF 30s were equipped with a Deutz F22 5.14 engine. Owned by Ted Sanger.

Howard DH 22

Manufacturer: Howard Auto Cultivators Ltd
Country of origin: Australia
Period of manufacture: 1928–52
Engine make: own
Fuel: petrol–kerosene
Cooling: water
Hp: 28 belt
Rpm: 1250
No. of cylinders: 4
Bore and stroke: 3.375 x 4.375in
Cubic capacity: 210cu in
Gears forward: 5 or 10
Gears reverse: 1 or 2
Drawbar pull: n/a
Weight: 4500lbs (with hoe)

Howard DH 22

A rugged tractor, normally sold with an attached rotary cultivator, the Howard DH 22 was rough to drive and was fitted with a hand crank only. This was the sole indigenous Australian farm tractor to be exported in quantity world-wide and proved popular in Cuba for working sugar plantations. Owned by Dudley and Dianne McDermott.

International Farmall F 12

Manufacturer: International Harvester Co.
Country of origin: USA
Period of manufacture: 1932–38
Engine make: own
Fuel: petrol–kerosene
Cooling: water
Hp: 16.2 brake
Rpm: 1400
No. of cylinders: 4
Bore and stroke: 3 x 4in
Cubic capacity: 113cu in
Gears forward: 3
Gears reverse: 1
Drawbar pull: 1870 at 2.34mph
Weight: 2700lbs

International Farmall F 12

The baby of the 1930s Farmall F series, the F 12 was a trouble-free, under-stressed, capable row cropper but had an unbelievably uncomfortable driving position plus a dangerous braking system with dual pull-on hand levers. The tricycle configuration was intended for level country only.

In February 1951 this advertisement appeared in Australia's New South Wales *Agricultural Gazette*. The Farmall Super A hydraulic system was emphasised in an attempt to counter the increasing compe-tition from Ferguson. Despite showing its age in 1951, the Farmall Super A was still a very desirable lightweight tractor. The offset engine provided excellent vision of the furrow when ploughing.

International Farmall Super A

The Super A, of which 90 000 were produced, was but one variant of the A series, the world's top-selling lightweight tractor in the 1940s. The arrival of Ferguson's hydraulic system in Ford and Ferguson tractors hastened the end of the Farmall dominance. Owned by Wayne and Bob Jensen.

International Farmall Super A

Manufacturer. International Harvester Co.
Country of origin: USA
Period of manufacture: 1939–54*
Engine make: own
Fuel: petrol–kerosene
Cooling: water
Hp: 19.06 belt
Rpm: 1400
No. of cylinders: 4
Bore and stroke: 3 x 4in
Cubic capacity: 113cu in
Gears forward: 4
Gears reverse: 1
Drawbar pull: 2360lbs at 1.97mph
Weight: 2385lbs
All A series variants were manufactured during this period.

Ivel

This was one of the world's earliest lightweight tractors, produced in the first decade of the 20th century, when the trend by other pioneer tractor designers was to heavyweights, following the pattern of the big steamers. Importantly, the Ivel worked well and had a degree of reliability uncommon in the era. A number were exported to the USA and other parts of the world. Owned by Norm McKenzie. *(Courtesy M Daw)*

Ivel

Manufacturer: Ivel Agricultural Motors Ltd
Country of origin: England
Period of manufacture: 1902–16
Engine make: own*
Fuel: petrol
Cooling: water
Hp: 18 brake
Rpm: 850
No. of cylinders: 2
Bore and stroke: 5.5 x 6in
Cubic capacity: 177cu in
Gears forward: 1
Gears reverse: 1
Drawbar pull: equivalent to two horses
Weight: 3136lbs
Later models powered by Aster, then Payne and Bates, engines.

John Deere L (styled)

Manufacturer: Deere & Co.
Country of origin: USA
Period of manufacture: 1937–46
Engine make: Hercules NXB*
Fuel: petrol
Cooling: water
Hp: 10.42 belt
Rpm: 1480
No. of cylinders: 2
Bore and stroke: 3.25 x 4in
Cubic capacity: 66cu in
Gears forward: 3
Gears reverse: 1
Drawbar pull: 1235lbs at 2mph
Weight: 1550lbs
Fitted with a JD engine from serial No. 640000 on.

John Deere L (styled)

The Model L was aimed specifically at converting small-holding farmers who still used a single horse to the technology of a tractor, and it proved to be a suitable and inexpensive alternative. It also was ideal as a utility tractor on larger properties. Unlike most John Deere tractors, the model L featured vertical cylinders. Owned by Ab Brimblecombe.

LHB Model LH 5

Manufacturer: Linke-Hofman-Werke AG
Country of origin: Germany
Period of manufacture: 1949–54
Engine make: Henschel 515 DE
Fuel: diesel
Cooling: water
Hp: 22 brake
Rpm: 1800
No. of cylinders: 2
Bore and stroke: 90 x 125mm
Cubic capacity: 1590cc
Gears forward: 5
Gears reverse: 1
Drawbar pull: n/a
Weight: 1925kg

LHB Model LH 5

Common in a number of European lightweights, this example of an LHB was largely assembled from components sourced from other manufacturers. The heart of the unit was the 2-cylinder diesel engine produced by Henschel, a company with many years of automotive and aircraft manufacturing. Owned by A Latimore.

Lanz Bulldog D 1706

Manufacturer. Heinrich Lanz AG
Country of origin: Germany
Period of manufacture: 1952–55
Engine make: own (semidiesel)
Fuel: diesel
Cooling: water
Hp: 17 brake
Rpm: 950
No. of cylinders: 1 (2-stroke valve-less)
Bore and stroke: 130 x 170mm
Cubic capacity: 2260cc
Gears forward: 6
Gears reverse: 2
Drawbar pull: 3530lbs at 1.55mph
Weight: 1310kg

Lanz Bulldog D 1706

A brilliant tractor abounding in features, the Lanz Bulldog D 1706 was better than its replacement model, the D 1606. It was capable of an amazing drawbar pull for a 17hp unit, and fuel consumption was measured in mere pints! 3-point linkage included lift and down pressure, and it was also equipped with independent front-wheel suspension, push button pendulum start, belt pulley and lighting equipment. Owned by the author.

Newman AN 3

Manufacturer: Newman Industries Ltd*
Country of origin: England
Period of manufacture: 1948–52
Engine make: Coventry Victor
Fuel: petrol
Cooling: air
Hp: 11 belt
Rpm: n/a
No. of cylinders: 2**
Bore and stroke: n/a
Cubic capacity: 804cc
Gears forward: 3
Gears reverse: 1
Drawbar pull: 1500lbs at n/a
Weight: 1650lbs
*Previously Kendall.
**Also available was the Newman WD 2, powered by a 1-cylinder Coventry Victor diesel engine, and the AN 4, equipped with a 12hp, 2-cylinder Coventry Victor petrol engine or the optional 2-cylinder Enfield diesel.

Newman AN 3

The Newman AN 3 was an oddball disaster that did nothing for the integrity of the British tractor industry. No redeeming features have yet been discovered but, like all oddball tractors, today it is a very desirable icon in a collection. Owned by David Yates.

The engine which powered the original Ivel
tractors was a horizontally opposed 2-cylinder
unit designed by Dan Albone. It depended
largely upon drip feed lubrication and featured vacuum inlet valves. Later engines were
produced by Aster, then Payne and Bates,
which had push rod valves and a larger
capacity oil sump as part of the crank case.

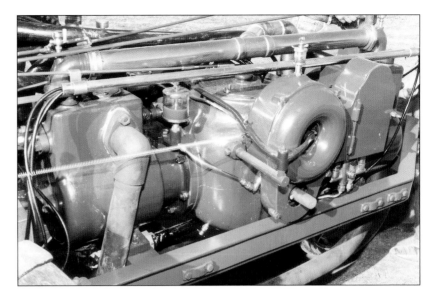

A Newman AN 3 Coventry Victor engine bay
with the horizontally opposed, 2-cylinder,
4-stroke 11hp engine.

The Nord ADN 25 had a 2-cylinder, 4-stroke
diesel engine capable of producing 30hp at
1800rpm.

Nord ADN 25

Manufacturer: Acieries du Nord
Country of origin: France
Period of manufacture: 1948–52
Engine make: Georges Irat
Fuel: diesel
Cooling: water
Hp: 30 belt
Rpm: 1800
No. of cylinders: 2
Bore and stroke: 4 x 4.9in
Cubic capacity: 2165cc
Gears forward: 3
Gears reverse: 1
Drawbar pull: 4100lbs at 2.4mph
Weight: 2970lbs

Nord ADN 25

An aggressive and purposeful diesel crawler, the ADN 25 was the baby of the Nord range and possibly the best. The low track profile could, however, prove a problem in boggy conditions. The unit was ideal for vineyard operation. Owned by Les Noll.

OTA Monarch

Manufacturer: Oak Tree Appliance Co. (Singer Motor Co. from 1953)
Country of origin: England
Period of manufacture: 1951–56
Engine make: Ford
Fuel: petrol
Cooling: water
Hp: 17 brake
Rpm: 2000
No. of cylinders: 4
Bore and stroke: 2.5 x 3.64in
Cubic capacity: 71.4cu in
Gears forward: 6
Gears reverse: 2
Drawbar pull: 2000lbs at 2mph*
Weight: 1430lbs
Manufacturer's claim—almost certainly over-optimistic.

OTA Monarch

Although a vast improvement over its 3-wheeled predecessor, the Monarch's only claim to glory was that it looked cuddly and was perfect for driving to the front gate to pick up the mail! This example, owned by Barbara Puls, is the envy of other collectors owing to its rarity and uniqueness. *(Courtesy U Schultz)*

Porsche Standard Star

Manufacturer: Porsche-Diesel-Motorenbau
Country of origin: Germany
Period of manufacture: 1960–63
Engine make: own
Fuel: diesel
Cooling: air
Hp: 30 brake
Rpm: 2300
No. of cylinders: 2
Bore and stroke: 98 x 116mm
Cubic capacity: 1750cc
Gears forward: 8
Gears reverse: 2
Drawbar pull: n/a
Weight: 1520kg

Porsche Standard Star

Cutting edge technology was used in this classic German package, and the inclusion of a fluid clutch and creeper gears make it unbeatable in the Slow Race category at classic tractor rallies. The air-cooled, 4-stroke diesel engine is worthy of the famous Ferdinand Porsche name. Formerly of the Hartmut Kiehn Collection.

Rumely Do All

Manufacturer: Advance-Rumely Thresher Co.
Country of origin: USA
Period of manufacture: 1928–31
Engine make: Waukesha
Fuel: petrol
Cooling: water
Hp: 21.6 brake
Rpm: 1400
No. of cylinders: 4
Bore and stroke: 3.5 x 4.5in
Cubic capacity: n/a
Gears forward: 2
Gears reverse: 1
Drawbar pull: 2012lbs at 3.04mph
Weight: 3702lbs

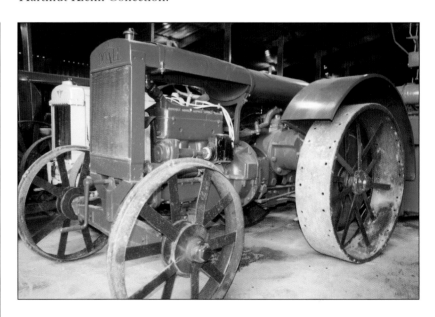

Rumely Do All

The lightweight member of the Rumely Oil Pull family, the Do All was actually a rebadged Toro, the name of the tractor company which Rumely purchased in 1928. It was sold in opposition to the Fordson F, but at twice the price. 3192 were built. A rare collectable artefact outside the USA. Owned by Ab Brimblecombe.

Same 12 HP

Manufacturer: Soc. Anonima Motori Endothermic
Country of origin: Italy
Period of manufacture: 1948–50
Engine make: own
Fuel: petrol–kerosene
Cooling: air
Hp: 12 brake
Rpm: 1200
No. of cylinders: 1
Bore and stroke: n/a
Cubic capacity: n/a
Gears forward: 6
Gears reverse: 2
Drawbar pull: n/a
Weight: n/a

Same 12 HP

This compact Italian classic was equipped with a 2-stage clutch and live pto shaft, plus high and low ratio gearbox and turning brakes. It was one of the first Same models after the company name was changed from Cassani in 1942. Owned by Tony Clements. *(Courtesy T Clements)*

Steyr 80

Manufacturer: Steyr-Daimler-Puch
Country of origin: Austria
Period of manufacture: 1950–n/a
Engine make: own
Fuel: diesel
Cooling: water
Hp: 15 brake
Rpm: 1600
No. of cylinders: 1
Bore and stroke: 110 x 140mm
Cubic capacity: 1330cc
Gears forward: 4
Gears reverse: 1
Drawbar pull: 1872lbs at 1.8mph
Weight: 1200kg

Steyr 80

Of all the fine European lightweights, this Austrian tractor had to be one of the best. Its low centre of gravity and weight distribution resulted in it being a favourite with Alpine farmers. Advanced hydraulics and 3-point linkage were standard equipment. Owned by Ted Sanger.

Stihl 144

Manufacturer: Andreas Stihl Maschinenfabrik
Country of origin: Germany
Period of manufacture: 1954–59
Engine make: own (2-stroke)
Fuel: diesel
Cooling: air
Hp: 14 brake
Rpm: 1890
No. of cylinders: 1
Bore and stroke: 90 x 120mm
Cubic capacity: 763cc
Gears forward: 5
Gears reverse: 1
Drawbar pull: n/a
Weight: 750kg

Stihl 144

Better known for its range of chainsaws, Stihl introduced the 144 into a very competitive European market in 1954. Rebadged versions were sold in France as both CGM 14 and Laffly 140. Although not a row cropper in the strict sense, commercial vegetable farmers appreciated the high clearance. The 144 was a basic yet well-appointed lightweight with good performance from its 14hp engine. Owned by Howard Pryor.

Stock Raupenstock

Manufacturer: Stock u Co. AG
Country of origin: Germany
Period of manufacture: 1924–29
Engine make: Deutz
Fuel: petrol–kerosene
Cooling: water
Hp: 28 brake
Rpm: 1000
No. of cylinders: 2
Bore and stroke: 120 x 160mm
Cubic capacity: 3617cc
Gears forward: 3
Gears reverse: 1
Drawbar pull: 3500 at 2mph
Weight: 4850lbs

Stock Raupenstock

An unusually designed crawler, the Raupenstock featured front-axle drive, resulting in almost the entire weight being over the drivers. This provided outstanding traction and a creditable drawbar pull for a 1924 tractor of 28hp. Its makers alleged it could handle a 5-furrow plough, but obviously in soft soil. It was inclined to throw tracks in aggressive, tight turns.

THE 28 H.P. STOCK ENDLESS CHAIN TRACTOR
FRONT WHEEL DRIVE
Spare Parts Readily Obtained in Sydney.
No chain supporting rollers.

Runs on kerosene.

Fuel consumption low.

All working parts easily accessible.

Two adjustable drawbars.

Belt pulley, 11in. diam. 1000 r.p.m.

Turning radius about 6ft.

The High-power Tractor for all Work.

A light, high-power machine weighing 4850 lbs., including fuel and water, and gives a drawbar pull of 3500 lbs. in first gear, which is the equivalent of 15 average farm horses.

Three forward speeds—1st 2 m.p.h.; 2nd, 3 m.p.h.; 3rd, 5 m.p.h.—Reverse.

Owing to the weight of this machine being over the front or driving axle, any overloading does not lift the front wheels, but merely pushes the back wheels further into the ground, thus increasing the road grip with the load. This, together with the fact that the initial road grip and thrust is derived from the **Front** end of the chain, keeps the full length of the chain on the ground, thus giving 100 per cent. road grip and tractive efficiency.

Price £495 Complete

Chain pins and eye holes in chain links specially protected from dust and consequent excessive wear by soft steel bushing caps.

Full details and specifications of this machine will be forwarded on request by Sole Australasian Distributors:

This advertisement for Stock tractors appeared in Australian rural newspapers in 1928.

Wallis Cub Junior model J
Manufacturer: Wallis Tractor Co.*
Country of origin: USA
Period of manufacture: 1915–16
Engine make: own
Fuel: petrol
Cooling: water
Hp: 25 belt
Rpm: 900
No. of cylinders: 4
Bore and stroke: 4.25 x 5.75in
Cubic capacity: n/a
Gears forward: 2
Gears reverse: 1
Drawbar pull: 2600lbs at 2.5mph
Weight: 3345lbs
Acquired by JI Case Plow Works in 1919.

Wallis Cub Junior model J

The author at the wheel of the world's first boiler plate unit construction (as opposed to girder frame). The Cub Junior was a genuine lightweight when compared to its big brother, the massive Wallis Bear, and was recognised as a milestone in the evolution of the American tractor. A dependable performer, the Cub Junior was credited with converting many small holders to tractor technology. Displayed at the Western Development Museum, Saskatchewan, Canada. *(Courtesy M Daw)*

Leave it to Ludwig

In 1955 I was invited to join the newly established Lanz Australia Pty Ltd as a field representative. The job involved assisting the company's country-based dealers in marketing Lanz Bulldog tractors, organising displays at country agricultural shows and staging tractor field days. At the same time I was charged with keeping a watchful eye on the opposition. Accordingly, most of my time was spent in the field either with farmers or dealers. Every few weeks I returned to the Sydney head office for a short break and to brief the managing director, Hans Tronser, on developments occurring in the rural areas. I also took these opportunities to discuss technical developments with Ludwig Simon, the chief engineer. The following is an account of an eventful two days in October 1955.

I was enjoying my breakfast of bacon and eggs, for which the Globe hotel at Cootamundra was noted, when word came that there was a phone call for me. The call was from an uncharacteristically stressed John Ross-Reid, my Lanz dealer based in Leeton, some 257 kilometres west of Cootamundra. He was clearly agitated and urged me to drop everything and proceed to Leeton with all haste as he had a crisis on his hands.

It appeared that a Mr Bossley, a prominent farmer in the region, was about to purchase two tractors for his share farmer. He had narrowed the field down and decided he would buy either two new Fordson Major Diesels or two Lanz Bulldog D3606. John Ross-Reid explained that a comparative on-site demonstration of the two competing tractors had taken place the previous day at Mr Bossley's farm. Everyone, including Mr Bossley, had anticipated that the German tractor would have decidedly outperformed the Fordson. But not so; the Fordson Major had pulled Mr Bossley's scarifier a gear faster than the Lanz.

John explained to me that he had persuaded Mr Bossley to delay signing an order for the Fordsons until an expert had checked out the Lanz. He had been given twenty-four hours to prove the Lanz was the more able tractor, or Mr Bossley would purchase two Fordsons.

The villages of Coolamon, Matong, Grong Grong, and the town of Narrandera flashed by in a blur as I urged the not-yet run-in Morris Isis to the hitherto unexplored top end of the speedometer, whilst I powered on towards Leeton. It was unthinkable that a Lanz D3606 had been outdone by a Fordson!

In my capacity with Lanz, I was not supposed to be a technical type but in truth I had a fair amount of mechanical knowledge about the product range. I also did most of the demonstrating, so there was no doubt in my mind that I would be able to rectify the problem and retrieve the sale for John Ross-Reid.

I charged the locust-splattered Isis into Mr Bossley's yard and came to a skidding halt, creating an unappreciated cloud of dust. There they were, impatiently awaiting my arrival: John, Mr Bossley, his share farmer, a smug looking Fordson dealer and half a dozen people who had drifted in to watch the fun. The Lanz was already hitched to the trailed McCormick 10-foot scarifier, so it remained for me to climb on board and start the engine.

As soon as I notched the tractor into gear and moved off, I knew there was a problem. An hour later, having checked the atomiser, fuel pump, the fuel itself and the governor controls, the tractor still lacked grunt. Mr Bossley was not amused. John Ross-Reid looked grim. My reputation had gone into decline. Only the Fordson dealer found joy in the proceedings and had his order book at the ready.

I sensed Mr Bossley secretly wanted the Lanz to outgun the Fordson. So he raised no objection when I requested I use the homestead telephone to call Ludwig Simon in the head office in Sydney.

Ludwig Simon is simply the most brilliant tractor technician I have ever encountered in half a century of working with tractors. Ramrod straight and with piercing eyes, he commanded respect in any place which was honoured by his presence. In 1955, all that Ludwig had missing was a Wehrmacht Colonel's uniform.

'No! It is not possible,' he bellowed down the phone to me, in his parade ground, heavily accented voice.

'Ludwig, I can assure you this D3606 is gutless, and,' I reiterated, 'the Fordson is totally outperforming it.' There was a snort, followed by a pause.

'You will meet me at the airport tomorrow morning,' he instructed. Then more kindly he added, 'You will not concern yourself. I shall rectify the problem.' With that the phone went dead.

Ludwig's flight touched down at the local airport the next morning. The rear door opened and the steps unfolded. The captain, followed by the second officer and hostess, alighted and together they formed a sort of guard of honour for the disembarking passengers, a customary airline procedure in those graceful days. In this instance, the sole passenger was Ludwig.

So there he was, alighting from what could have been mistaken for his personal flight and being saluted by the crew. In the style of a true Teutonic aristocrat, he merely gave a curt nod in response and strode over to where I was waiting with the Morris Isis. He remained by the side of the car, leaving me in no doubt that I was expected to open the rear door for him in the manner of a corporal ushering his colonel into a military staff car.

We swept into Mr Bossley's yard and the great Ludwig Simon emerged into the sunlight from the rear of the car. By now, word of the Lanz problem had spread around. Not only had everyone who was present the previous day returned, but it appeared the entire community had arrived to witness what was now an event of major significance and certainly great entertainment.

I formally introduced Ludwig to the assembly. He clicked his well polished heels and gave a slight bow—then frowned when nobody applauded. His frown turned to a withering stare when some well-intended fellow called out, 'Good on you, mate.' As we approached the errant tractor I attempted to describe the problem, but Ludwig dismissed my comments with a wave of his hand. 'It is of no concern,' he informed me.

John Ross-Reid grimaced as Ludwig banged his briefcase onto the bonnet of his beautifully polished, scratch-free Wolseley. Ludwig then proceeded to extract a starched, gleaming white dustcoat, which he put on over his suit. Exclamations of incredulity and amazement came from the gathered crowd. Ludwig's gimlet eye flashed around the assembly, seeking out the culprits. Silence reigned, order was restored.

Ludwig then produced a highly polished spanner from a small leather

John Ross-Reid, photographed by Ludwig Simon in 1955, demonstrates a Lanz Bulldog Model H. He had a tremendous following in the district and regularly topped the Lanz sales in his State. *(Courtesy L Simon)*

This interesting photo was taken on 29 July 1950. The location was a government farm an hour's drive north of the Indian capital New Delhi. An anxious Ludwig Simon (second from right) is endeavouring to convey to the driver the necessity of immediately applying the clutch. The Lanz Bulldog has become bogged and is in the process of digging itself into the ground. Ludwig's problem is that he cannot simply take over the controls by elbowing the driver out of the seat, as he (the driver) is no less an exalted figure than the Indian Minister of Supply, Sri Harekrusha Mahtab.
(Courtesy H Simon)

case which he carried in his inside breast pocket. He proceeded to make adjustments to the governor and the fuel pump, the covers having first been removed by John Ross-Reid. Nobody could precisely see what actual adjustments were made.

Ludwig signalled for me to start the engine. He then delighted the fascinated and, by now, highly intrigued audience by introducing a stethoscope into the proceedings, which gave him the appearance of a visiting neurosurgeon. He sounded the engine with the stethoscope and nodded his head knowingly. Then, abruptly, he removed the still-immaculate dustcoat and placed both it and the stethoscope back into the briefcase. He turned to me and announced, 'Now we shall go.' I must have looked amazed.

'But Ludwig, until we test the tractor how do we know it's fixed?' I dared to ask. Ludwig looked at me with disdain as if examining some lower form of pond life. He seemed to be considering whether perpetual confinement to barracks was adequate punishment or if I should simply be taken out and shot. However, he finally just shrugged and indicated that if I really thought it necessary I could test the tractor myself.

Owing to the vastness of my Lanz territory, I regularly covered over 120 000 kilometres every nine months in my company vehicle, by which time it had largely self-destructed and I would be issued with a replacement. The vehicle which proved itself to be more robust than most was this 6-cylinder, 2.6 litre Morris Isis. Note the details on the signboard.

There is little else to tell. As I expected, the Lanz Bulldog D3606 sped around the paddock like a young colt, dragging the scarifier behind. I could even notch it into fourth gear, and it completely outshone the performance of the Fordson Major Diesel.

The show was over and Mr Bossley was pleased and relieved to have his initial confidence in the Lanz confirmed. John Ross-Reid unscrewed the cap of his fountain pen in preparation for the signing of the order. The Fordson dealer departed in a huff. Ludwig Simon and I adjourned to the Leeton Hydro Hotel for a round or two of schnapps followed by a leisurely lunch. Yes those were great days, when the countryside was full of fascinating characters and selling tractors was fun!

1955 Fordson Major Diesel
Manufacturer: Ford Motor Co. Ltd
Country of origin: England
Engine type: 4-cyl. compression ignition diesel
Hp: 39.4 belt
Rpm: 1600
Bore and stroke: 3.937 x 4.528in
Displacement: 3.6L
Compression ratio: 16 to 1
Gears forward: 6
Gears reverse: 2
Drawbar pull: 5313lbs at 1.73mph
Weight: 3.174 tons (with cast rims)

1955 Lanz Bulldog D3606
Manufacturer: Heinrich Lanz AG
Country of origin: Germany
Engine type: 1-cyl. 2-stroke valveless semidiesel
Hp: 36 belt
Rpm: 1050
Bore and stroke: 150 x 210mm
Displacement: 3.7L
Compression ratio: 11 to 1
Gears forward: 6
Gears reverse: 2
Drawbar pull: 6200lbs at 1.7mph
Weight: 3.2 tons

'Leave it to Ludwig' first appeared in condensed form in the November 2002 issue of the *Australian Cotton Grower*.

Heavyweights

The very first tractors were heavyweights. With a philosophy determined by the dictates of steam traction engines, trailblazer tractor designers clung to the belief that 'heavy is beautiful'. Englishmen D Albone and HP Saunderson were the first to comprehend that the new internal combustion-engine driven tractors did not have to replicate the steamers to be efficient.

Despite the gradual but inevitable swing to lighter tractors, there always remained a need for the heavyweights, which were capable of tackling the big jobs. Keeping pace with advancing engine technology, horsepower of the big muscle machines increased from around 30hp at the beginning of the 20th century to a figure approaching 1000hp 100 years later.

Not surprisingly, the majority of the heavyweights emanated from the drawing boards of North American and Soviet tractor designers. The endless prairies of the USA, Canada and Russia were the perfect procreating grounds for wide implements and big tractors.

The term heavyweight is of course subjective. A big tractor to a Dutch market gardener would be seen as diminutive by a Pampas farmer in Argentina. The David Brown 50 TD crawler was considered large by those who owned a David Brown 30 TD in the 1950s, yet in 1920 the Holt Caterpillar 5-ton was merely a lightweight compared to the Caterpillar 10-ton.

Accordingly, in this chapter the term heavyweight is not entirely determined by physical mass or drawbar pull capabilities of the tractors discussed, but rather by how a particular model of tractor would have been perceived by farmers in the region in which it was purchased and used.

The few tractors examined here represent a mere fraction of the total. Heavyweights reviewed elsewhere within the book are not included in this chapter.

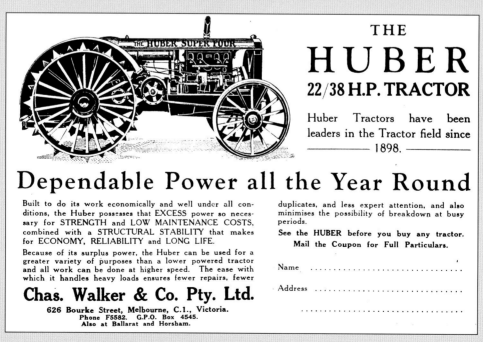

This Huber advertisement, which appeared in 1928, emphasised the company's years of tractor experience, reinforced with claims designed to promote confidence in the mind of the buyer. Curiously, unlike most tractor advertisements of the 1920s, it provides no specifications.

Aultman Taylor 30-60

Old-timers say this was the pick of the early prairie tractors. When tested at Nebraska in 1920, it was discovered that the manufacturer's rating of 60 belt hp had been understated—the true figure being 80 belt hp. The big engine was easy to start and from a driver's view point the tractor was user friendly—a rarity in those days. This 1916 example is owned by Dan Ehlerding, Ohio.

Aultman Taylor 30-60

Manufacturer: Aultman Taylor Machinery Co.
Country of origin: USA
Period of manufacture: 1911–1923
Engine make: own
Fuel: petrol–kerosene
Cooling: water
Hp: 80 belt
Rpm: 500
No. of cylinders: 4
Bore and stroke: 7 x 9in
Cubic capacity: n/a
Gears forward: 1
Gears reverse: 1
Drawbar pull: 9160lbs at 2.38mph
Weight: 24 450lbs

Case 25-45 Crossmount

Although only the second largest of the Crossmounts, the 25-45 was a formidable opponent at tractor trials. During its short production life only 980 were made. Like all Crossmounts, the tractor was a handful to drive and its ability was limited by having only two forward gears, but it was a dependable and trouble-free tractor. Displayed at the Gunnedah Rural Museum, Australia.

Case 25-45 Crossmount

Manufacturer: JI Case Threshing Machine Co.
Country of origin: USA
Period of manufacture: 1925–1928
Engine make: own
Fuel: petrol–kerosene
Cooling: water
Hp: 52.59 belt
Rpm: 850
No. of cylinders: 4
Bore and stroke: 5.50 x 6.75in
Cubic capacity: n/a
Gears forward: 2
Gears reverse: 1
Drawbar pull: 5750lbs at 2.14mph
Weight: 10 180lbs

This advertisement for Case Crossmount tractors appeared in the *American Exporter* in August 1928.

Clayton 40 Chain Rail

Following the production of 500 35hp crawlers, commissioned by the British Food Production Department, the tractor was upgraded to an improved 40hp version. Band brakes were activated by the steering wheel for directional changes, but could also be applied independently for normal braking purposes. *(Clayton & Shuttleworth promotional material)*

Clayton 40 Chain Rail

Manufacturer: Clayton & Shuttleworth Ltd
Country of origin: England
Period of manufacture: 1922
Engine make: Dorman
Fuel: petrol-kerosene
Cooling: water
Hp: 40 brake
Rpm: 1200
No. of cylinders: 4
Bore and stroke: n/a
Cubic capacity: 384cu in
Gears forward: 2
Gears reverse: 1
Drawbar pull: 4780lbs at 2mph
Weight: n/a

Chamberlain Super 90

A classic in its time. In terms of sheer grunt, the Super 90 was possibly the most powerful 2-wheel drive farm tractor in its era. A total of 773 were produced. The high cost of manufacture contributed to the financial difficulties of Chamberlain Industries, ultimately resulting in a takeover by Deere & Co. of Moline. Owned by the author.

Chamberlain Super 90

Manufacturer: Chamberlain Industries Ltd
Country of origin: Australia
Period of manufacture: 1962–1966
Engine make: GM Detroit
Fuel: diesel
Cooling: water
Hp: 100
Rpm: 1800
No. of cylinders: 3 (supercharged 2-stroke)
Bore and stroke: 4.5 x 5in
Cubic capacity: 213cu in
Gears forward: 9
Gears reverse: 3
Drawbar pull: 8406lbs at 3.1mph
Weight: 6.5 tons*
With water ballasted 23.1 x 26 rear tyres and heavy duty rims.

Cockshutt 90

Manufacturer: Oliver Corporation
Country of origin: USA
Period of manufacture: 1937–1957
Engine make: Oliver
Fuel: petrol–kerosene
Cooling: water
Hp: 49.04 belt
Rpm: 1125
No. of cylinders: 4
Bore and stroke: 4.75 x 6.25in
Cubic capacity: 443cu in
Gears forward: 4*
Gears reverse: 1
Drawbar pull: 7594lbs at 2.9mph
Weight: 6760lbs
5 forward gears if originally fitted with pneumatic tyres.

Cockshutt 90

The Cockshutt Plow Company of Brantford, Ontario, sold rebadged Oliver tractors in Canada, painted in the Cockshutt livery of red and gold. The Cockshutt 90 was identical to the stalwart muscle machine the Oliver 90, sold in the USA and around the world. The Cockshutt earned a reputation for strength and legendary drawbar pull. This Cockshutt 90 was discovered in a private collection in British Columbia, Canada.

Commonsense 20-50

Manufacturer: Commonsense Gas Traction Co.
Country of origin: USA
Period of manufacture: 1917–1920
Engine make: Herschell-Spillman
Fuel: petrol–kerosene
Cooling: water
Hp: 50 belt
Rpm: 1200
No. of cylinders: 8
Bore and stroke: 3.25 x 5in
Cubic capacity: n/a
Gears forward: 2
Gears reverse: 1
Drawbar pull: n/a
Weight: 6700lbs

Commonsense 20-50

The world's first tractor fitted with a V8 engine was designed by HW Adams and produced in Minneapolis, USA. Adams ran tractor training schools which were well attended by enthusiastic young farmers. The power advantages of the V8 were emphasised by Adams, resulting in most of the Commonsense sales being made to his indoctrinated students. The unit had a single rear driving wheel, which dispensed with the necessity of a differential. *(Courtesy Brad Drury)*

CO-OP 3

Manufacturer: Duplex Machinery Co.
Country of origin: USA
Period of manufacture: 1938–1940
Engine make: Chrysler-Dodge
Fuel: petrol
Cooling: water
Hp: 40 brake*
Rpm: 2000
No. of cylinders: 6
Bore and stroke: 3.375 x 4.5in
Cubic capacity: 242cu in
Gears forward: 5
Gears reverse: 1
Drawbar pull: 2679lbs at 2.38mph*
Weight: 6065lbs
Owners frequently disconnected the governor, thus increasing hp to 80 at 3200rpm, and substantially adding to the drawbar pull and road speed.

CO-OP 3

In 1938 the CO-OP 3, the heavyweight of the range, was manufactured for The Farmers Union Central Exchange Co-operative of Minnesota, USA. Designed by Dent Parrett (of Parrett tractor fame) the CO-OP 3 used mainly Dodge truck running gears with a Clark gearbox. The unit could handle a 3-furrow plough, or haul a wagon into town at an ungoverned 45mph. Pictured is the author at the wheel of a CO-OP 3 owned by Jack Cochran of Indiana, USA. *(Courtesy M Daw)*

Deutz F3M 417

This was one of the last of the water-cooled models—and the largest. There were few tractors that could outpull this solidly engineered German thoroughbred. Beyond Europe, however, its pricing structure made it difficult to sell against the competition from the big American tractors. Photo is of Ron Keech driving his big Deutz at the Gunnedah Rural Museum, Australia.

Deutz F3M 417

Manufacturer: Klockner-Humbolt-Deutz AG
Country of origin: Germany
Period of manufacture: 1948–1952
Engine make: own
Fuel: diesel
Cooling: water
Hp: 50 brake
Rpm: 1350
No. of cylinders: 3
Bore and stroke: 120 x 170mm
Cubic capacity: 5760cc
Gears forward: 5
Gears reverse: 1
Drawbar pull: 6000lbs at 2mph
Weight: 4500kg

Dutra D4 KB

Produced in Budapest, the Dutra D4 KB was a 4-wheel drive heavyweight aimed at the Eastern European market, but particularly the broad grain fields of northeast Hungary. The Dutra origins can be traced back to the old HSCS tractor, which became the Red Star. Dutra eventually became part of the Raba Steiger group. The Dutra pictured is regularly exhibited at classic tractor rallies in New Zealand. Owned by Bill and Stuart Sanders.

Dutra D4 KB

Manufacturer: Dutra Tractor Works
Country of origin: Hungary
Period of manufacture: 1969–1972
Engine make: Csepel DT613.15*
Fuel: diesel
Cooling: water
Hp: 100 brake
Rpm: 1850
No. of cylinders: 6
Bore and stroke: 110 x 140mm
Cubic capacity: 7990cc
Gears forward: 10
Gears reverse: 2
Drawbar pull: n/a
Weight: 5100kg
Alternative—Perkins 6.354

Fiat 80R

Manufacturer: Fiat S.p.A.
Country of origin: Italy
Period of manufacture: 1963–1967
Engine make: own
Fuel: diesel
Cooling: water
Hp: 84.12 brake
Rpm: 1650
No. of cylinders: 4
Bore and stroke: 4.92 x 5.51in
Cubic capacity: 492cu in
Drawbar pull: 9887lbs* at 2.4mph
Gears forward: 5
Gears reverse: 1
Weight: 6.8 tons*
When equipped with 23.1 x 26 rears, cast heavy-duty rims and water ballast.

Fiat 80R

The largest of all the classic Fiat farm tractors, the 80R was more than capable of matching performance with the biggest of the American heavyweights. In collector's terms, it is a rare beast. With 23.1 x 26 rear tyres, its width was 8.5ft and with water ballast and cast rims it tipped the scales at around 7 tons. This as-yet unrestored Fiat 80R is owned by the author.

Froelich

Manufacturer: John Froelich
Country of origin: USA
Period of manufacture: 1892–1893
Engine make: Van Duzen Gas Engine Co.
Fuel: petrol
Cooling: water
Hp: 16 brake
Rpm: n/a
No. of cylinders: 1
Bore and stroke: 14 x 14in
Cubic capacity: 2155cu in
Gears forward: 1
Gears reverse: 1
Drawbar pull: n/a
Weight: n/a

Froelich

Generally credited with being the first internal combustion engine tractor capable of operating a belt and hauling a wagon. There is only speculation, however, as to whether it ever pulled a plough. The unit was built on a timber chassis and equipped with Robinson steam engine running gear. Photo is of a miniature Froelich.

Hanomag K50

Manufacturer: Hanomag Maschinbaw AG
Country of origin: Germany
Period of manufacture: 1935–1936
Engine make: own
Fuel: diesel
Cooling: water
Hp: 50 brake
Rpm: 1300
No. of cylinders: 4
Bore and stroke: 135 x 150mm
Cubic capacity: 8870cc
Gears forward: 3
Gears reverse: 1
Drawbar pull: 7200lbs at 1.9mph
Weight: 4390kg

Hanomag K50

During the 1930s, Hanomag diesel-powered crawlers were held in high esteem in Europe and many other centres throughout the world. They were magnificently engineered and a delight to drive compared to other crawlers of the time. The steering-wheel-actuated directional control was precise and required very little effort on behalf of the operator. Peter Desch owns the largest collection of vintage Hanomags outside Europe. His 1935 K50 has been totally restored.

Holt Caterpillar 45

Manufacturer: Holt Manufacturing Co.
Country of origin: USA
Period of manufacture: 1916–1919
Engine make: own
Fuel: petrol
Cooling: water
Hp: 45 brake
Rpm: 600
No. of cylinders: 4
Bore and stroke: 6 x 7in
Cubic capacity: n/a
Gears forward: 2
Gears reverse: 1
Drawbar pull: n/a
Weight: 1390lbs

Holt Caterpillar 45

Although by no means the largest of the Holt crawlers, the 45 was indeed a heavyweight. The power of the tractor was well beyond the expectations of its 45hp unit engine. However the petrol consumption was horrific and under severe load conditions could run to around 10 gallons per hour. One of many rare tractors exhibited at the Booleroo Steam and Traction Preservation Society of South Australia. Colin Becker is at the controls.

Huber 22-38

Manufacturer: Huber Manufacturing Co.
Country of origin: USA
Period of manufacture: 1928
Engine make: Stearns
Fuel: petrol–kerosene
Cooling: water
Hp: 43.15 brake
Rpm: 1000*
No. of cylinders: 4
Bore and stroke: 4.75 x 6.5in
Cubic capacity: n/a
Gears forward: 2
Gears reverse: 1
Drawbar pull: 5419lbs at 1.78mph
Weight: 8595lbs
Performance figures relate to the 18-36.

Huber 22-38

Huber entered the tractor arena in 1898 when it acquired the Van Duzen Company of Ohio, USA. The 22-38 was an upgrade of its predecessor the 18-36, and the use of a Stearns engine was a good choice, giving the tractor a reputation for reliability. The two forward speeds, common for the era, restricted its versatility with varying implements. Les Burns has restored this example to original condition.

International Titan Type D

Manufacturer: International Harvester Co.
Country of origin: USA
Period of manufacture: 1910–1914
Engine make: own
Fuel: petrol–kerosene
Cooling: water
Hp: 31.6 brake
Rpm: 240
No. of cylinders: 1
Bore and stroke: 10 x 15in
Cubic capacity: 1177cu in
Gears forward: 1
Gears reverse: 1
Drawbar pull: n/a
Weight: 18 200lbs

International Titan Type D

A total of 1575 of these heavyweights were produced. With the chassis constructed from 10-inch channel iron, these tractors were immensely rigid and free from flexing and mis-alignment, a common problem with the first tractors. Early in the production life of the Type D, the rectangular evaporative cooling tower was introduced and became a recognisable feature, distinguishing the Titan from its stable mate, the Mogul. Owned by Jesse Martin.

John Deere D (early)

The Model D enjoyed a longer production life than any other tractor, with 160 000 produced. The tractor was of unit construction (no chassis), the 2-cylinder horizontal engine and transmission housings being bolted together to form a single rigid unit. The success of the Model D can be attributed to its simplicity of design, economy of operation and its dependability. Pictured is Max Thornton's John Deere D 1926 Model with the 24in spoked flywheel.

John Deere D (early)

Manufacturer: Deere and Co.
Country of origin: USA
Period of manufacture: 1923–1953
Engine make: own
Fuel: petrol–kerosene
Cooling: water
Hp: 30.4 belt
Rpm: 800
No. of cylinders: 2
Bore and stroke: 6.5 x 7in*
Cubic capacity: 465cu in
Gears forward: 2
Gears reverse: 1
Drawbar pull: 3277lbs at 2.58mph
Weight: 4403lbs
Increased to 6.75 x 7in in late 1927.

Lanz Bull Model T (D6006)

The Lanz flagship of the 1950s, the Model T represented the end of an era. It featured the new push-button start, a flat headed alloy piston and an updated loop scavenging system. This was a true muscle machine, capable of outperforming any competitor. It was the last of the big Bulldogs and also the most powerful. Owned by Andy McClelland.

Lanz Bull Model T (D6006)

Manufacturer: Heinrich Lanz AG
Country of origin: Germany
Period of manufacture: 1955–1960
Engine make: own
Fuel: diesel
Cooling: water
Hp: 60 brake
Rpm: 800
No. of cylinders: 1
Bore and stroke: 190 x 260mm
Cubic capacity: 7370cc
Gears forward: 6*
Gears reverse: 2
Drawbar pull: 8085lbs** at 2.46mph
Weight: 7877lbs
The DT (D6016) had 9 forward and 3 reverse gears.
**Marburg test No. 117 was conducted with the T on 15 x 30 rear tyres. With 18 x 26 rears water ballasted and heavy duty cast rims (commonly fitted in Australia) the drawbar pull was increased to over 10 000lbs.*

Massey Ferguson 88

Manufacturer: Massey Ferguson Inc.
Country of origin: USA
Period of manufacture: 1960–1962
Engine make: Continental
Fuel: diesel
Cooling: water
Hp: 63.31 brake
Rpm: 2000
No. of cylinders: 4
Bore and stroke: 4 x 5.5in
Cubic capacity: 276.5cu in
Gears forward: 8
Gears reverse: 2
Drawbar pull: 8973lbs at 2.12mph
Weight: 12 133lbs—ballasted for test

Massey Ferguson 88

The MF 88, an updated version of the MF 85, was the first Massey Ferguson true heavyweight, replaced in 1962 by the Perkins-powered MF Super 90. The wide diameter 18 x 36 rear tyres enabled the tractor to apply its hp to the ground with minimal wheel slip. The MF 88 pictured is part of the extensive Shaw Collection in Westbury, Tasmania, Australia.

Massey Harris 25

Manufacturer: Massey Harris Co.
Country of origin: USA
Period of manufacture: 1933–1938
Engine make: own
Fuel: petrol–kerosene
Cooling: water
Hp: 48.25 belt
Rpm: 1200
No. of cylinders: 4
Bore and stroke: 4.375 x 5.75in
Cubic capacity: 346cu in
Gears forward: 4
Gears reverse: 1
Drawbar pull: 4501lbs at 2.2mph
Weight: 5385lbs

Massey Harris 25

The MH 25 is often confused with the MH Pacemaker. Both tractors had a similar profile but the MH 25 was, overall, larger with a bigger capacity engine. The original MH 25, introduced in 1933, was also known as the MH 3-4 Plow. It was a more pleasant tractor to drive than its main competitor, the International W30. Photo is of 1937 'styled' MH 25, part of the author's private collection.

Massey Harris 203

Manufacturer: Massey Harris Co.
Country of origin: USA
Period of manufacture: 1940–1947
Engine make: Continental
Fuel: petrol–kerosene
Cooling: water
Hp: 60 brake
Rpm: 2000
No. of cylinders: 6
Bore and stroke: 4 x 4.375in
Cubic capacity: 330cu in
Gears forward: 4
Gears reverse: 1
Drawbar pull: n/a
Weight: 6605lbs

Massey Harris 203

The MH 203 was never tested at Nebraska, due to the facility being mothballed during World War II. However, it was undoubtedly one of the most powerful farm tractors of the early 1940s. It was a sheer delight to operate, the big smooth 6-cylinder side valve engine providing an abundance of power. Only 1699 were produced. The MH 203 is relatively uncommon outside North America; this example is part of the author's private collection.

This 1937 Massey Harris advertisement illustrated the Pacemaker and the MH 25, both rebadged Wallis tractors. Curiously, they are both unstyled which suggests the distributor still had an inventory of superseded stock.

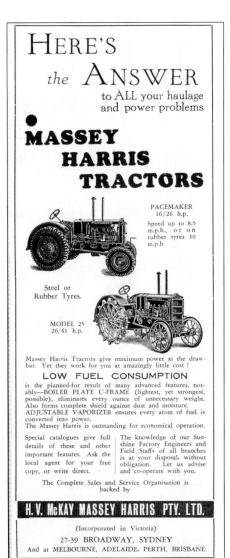

McClaren Diesel Oil-Engined Windlass

Manufacturer: J & H McClaren Ltd
Country of origin: England
Period of manufacture: 1930–1932
Engine make: McClaren Benz
Fuel: diesel
Cooling: water
Hp: 70 brake
Rpm: 800
No. of cylinders: 4 (supercharged)
Bore and stroke: n/a
Cubic capacity: n/a
Gears forward: 1
Gears reverse: 1
Drawbar pull: n/a
Weight: 9 tons

McClaren Diesel Oil-Engined Windlass

This was a tractor custom-built for cable winch ploughing. The vertical winding drum (as distinct from the horizontal drum) was a clever design feature shared with Bomford of Worcestershire. There was little chance of the cable 'falling off'. The cross-mount engine was also a distinctive McClaren feature for this type of tractor. It was started by a 2-cylinder, 8hp pilot engine. Sketch shows a McClaren mounted on Sawah patented wheels, which bridged the gap between conventional wheels and tracks.

McDonald EB

Manufacturer: AH McDonald & Co.
Country of origin: Australia
Period of manufacture: 1911–1915
Engine make: own
Fuel: petrol
Cooling: water
Hp: 20
Rpm: 650
No. of cylinders: 2
Bore and stroke: 6.25 x 8.25in*
Cubic capacity: n/a
Gears forward: 3
Gears reverse: 1
Drawbar pull: n/a
Weight: 3.5 tons
Increased in 1912 to 7.5 x 8.25in.

McDonald EB

Alfred Henry McDonald introduced the EB in 1911. The reputation of this crude but well-engineered tractor established the credentials of AH McDonald & Company as a manufacturer of tractors that, in those early days, compared favourably with its more established North American counterparts. Undoubtedly one of the world's rarest classic tractors is John Kirkpatrick's 1912 EB. (*Courtesy J Kirkpatrick*)

Sift TD 4

The TD 4 was fundamentally a commendable heavyweight tractor, but had ill-considered gear ratios, inadequate rear tyre equipment and an over-optimistic set of performance figures featured in its sales literature. It was, however, rugged with a typically (for the period) under-stressed, heavily built diesel engine. This interesting French classic has been elegantly restored by its owner, Mel Thomas. *(Courtesy M Thomas)*

Sift TD 4

Manufacturer: Tracteurs Sift
Country of origin: France
Period of manufacture: 1948–1954
Engine make: own
Fuel: diesel
Cooling: water
Hp: 38 belt*
Rpm: 1200
No. of cylinders: 4
Bore and stroke: 4.1875 x 6.3125in
Cubic capacity: n/a
Gears forward: 5
Gears reverse: 1
Drawbar pull: 4850lbs* at 2.2mph
Weight: 7840lbs
These figures differ with Sift literature but are in accordance with Australian Tractor Test No. 22 conducted in November 1951.

Twin City 27-44

The Twin City 27-44 was virtually a Twin City 20-35 with a higher hp rating. The engine featured four valves per cylinder, a design first appearing in 1920 in the Twin City 12-20. The 27-44 was noisy and heavy to steer and, with only two forward gears, the big tractor could never quite achieve its potential. Despite these shortcomings, Twin City tractors were magnificently engineered and capable of constant heavy work. The 1926 Twin City 27-44 pictured is at the Victorian Swan Hill Settlement, Australia. Newton Williams is driving.

Twin City 27-44

Manufacturer: Minneapolis Steel & Mach. Co.*
Country of origin: USA
Period of manufacture: 1926–1935
Engine make: own
Fuel: petrol-kerosene
Cooling: water
Hp: 49.05 brake
Rpm: 900
No. of cylinders: 4
Bore and stroke: 5.5 x 6.75in
Cubic capacity: n/a
Gears forward: 2
Gears reverse: 1
Drawbar pull: 5640 at 2.3mph
Weight: 10 500lbs
Following a merger in 1929– Minneapolis Moline Power Implement Co.

Vickers 15-30

Manufacturer: Vickers (Crayford) Ltd
Country of origin: England
Period of manufacture: 1925–1930
Engine make: own
Fuel: petrol–kerosene
Cooling: water
Hp: 30 brake
Rpm: 1000
No. of cylinders: 4
Bore and stroke: 4.5 x 6in
Cubic capacity: 381cu in
Gears forward: 3
Gears reverse: 1
Drawbar pull: n/a
Weight: n/a

Vickers 15-30

Vickers had an arrangement with International to produce a McCormick 15-30 copy under the Vickers name. The entire tractor was manufactured at the Vickers facility in Kent, England. Originally released as the Vickers Aussie, the 'Aussie' was dropped and the design progressively improved. The Vickers pictured is displayed at the Pioneer Park Museum, Parkes, Australia.

The articles below appeared in the October 1926 edition of *Power Farming in Australia*.

"TWIN CITY"

OVER three years ago we were looking for a tractor agency. Several offered. Amongst these the TWIN CITY alone possessed what were, in our opinion, certain fundamental features, both in the machine and in the organisation behind it. Firstly, the manufacturers were old-established, and had been successfully marketing tractors in the U.S.A. for a very long time. Even in Australia there are still in use two 40-65 TWIN CITIES, which were imported about 1912. Secondly, the manufacturers were content to rate their machines conservatively and not try to sell them at their "all-out" ratings.

Thirdly, the design of the TWIN CITY—especially in regard to its engine and transmission — followed closely the lines which had been evolved and proved through many millions of cars and trucks. We felt that here was something built on sound engineering principles, nothing freakish nor too radical, but up-to-date. When we noticed too, that the present design had not been changed in its essential features since 1918, we felt confident that in the TWIN CITY we could offer the New South Wales farmer something which was not so old as to be behind the times, nor yet so new as to be only an experiment. It is significant that nearly all the tractors put on the market in the last few years closely copy the TWIN CITY Engine design, although few have all its refinements, such as full pressure feed lubrication, three main bearings, counterbalanced crankshaft, and so on.

Mr. R. A. Malloch, Managing Director of Dangar, Gedye & Co. Ltd.

Vickers Tractor

ONCE again the Editor of "Power Farming" has kindly asked me to write something with regard to the Vickers 15-30 h.p. Tractor.

Five Points stand out clearly with regard to this Tractor, and I will deal with them briefly in the space available.

1. The Vickers Tractor is built of the highest quality British material, made and manufactured by a firm with a world-wide reputation as engineers.

2. The Vickers Tractor has been built in conjunction with the advice and suggestions of practical Australian farmers, who understand thoroughly the conditions under which the tractor will have to work.

3. The Vickers Tractor is equipped with and has the exclusive use of the Kendell-James Wheel, an Australian invention, which gives a positive grip under all conditions of soil surface.

4. The Vickers Tractor is built to give long service under all conditions with a minimum of running costs and repairs.

5. By purchasing Vickers Tractors you keep your trade within the Empire.

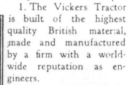
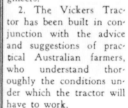
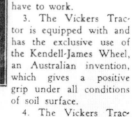

Sir Keith Smith, K.B.E., Representing Vickers Ltd., London.

Wallis Bear

Conceived in 1902, the Wallis Bear was first produced in 1906. Only nine units were made, the final one in 1912. The design of this giant tractor was well ahead of its time. It featured a pressure-lubricated, 4-cylinder ohv engine, power steering, individual turning brakes, sprung rear axle, plate spring-loaded clutch, all-speed governor and 3-speed fully enclosed transmission. Pictured is the world's only remaining Wallis Bear and the third built. Restored by EF Schmidt of Ohio, USA.

Wallis Bear

Manufacturer: Wallis Tractor Co.
Country of origin: USA
Period of manufacture: 1906–1912*
Engine make: own
Fuel: petrol–kerosene
Cooling: water
Hp: 50 belt
Rpm: 650
No. of cylinders: 4
Bore and stroke: 7.5 x 9in
Cubic capacity: 1480cu in
Gears forward: 3
Gears reverse: 1
Drawbar pull: 10 x furrow plough
Weight: 10.5 tons
A line of smaller hp Wallis Bears also became available.

The early Marshalls

With a history of manufacturing extending back to 1848, William Marshall Sons & Company of Gainsborough, Lincolnshire, England, welcomed the dawning of the 20th century with confidence and vision. The company had already established its credentials worldwide for engineering excellence; Marshall stationery steam engines and steam traction engines were performing agricultural, industrial, military and municipal assignments in distant places from Argentina to Alaska, from China to Cuba. But the majority of Marshall machines were sold into British Commonwealth countries, often obtaining favourable tariff concessions and thus enjoying a sales price advantage over North American and European competitors.

THE MARSHALL COLONIALS

It was not until 1906 that Marshall produced its first prototype tractor with an internal combustion engine. The power unit was a 2-cylinder petrol engine designed by Herbert Bamber—a highly respected engineer better known for his association with Vauxhall Motor Company. Bamber's tractor engine had a 7 x 7in bore and stroke and developed 30hp.

Pulling dual 2-furrow ploughs, the tractor was able to plough one acre each hour; it was normal in Britain for a pair of draught horses to plough one acre *per day* with the commonly used single-furrow mouldboard plough. The results obtained from the Bamber-engined prototype were therefore considered highly satisfactory.

By around 1910, Marshall had developed two tractor engines based upon the original prototype. A 2-cylinder version produced 30-35 brake hp and a 4-cylinder unit was rated at 60–70 brake hp.

Ultimately there were five classes of Marshall Colonials, the name given to these tractors. They were:

- Class C—2-cylinder 35 brake hp, one forward gear
- Class E—2-cylinder 35 brake hp, two forward gears
- Class D—4-cylinder 70 brake hp, one forward gear
- Class F—4-cylinder 70 brake hp, two forward gears
- Class G—4-cylinder 70 brake hp, two forward gears (sprung front axle).

The Class G was designed for heavy road haulage applications. It also proved an ideal unit for travelling showmen, as the big tractor, apart from its towing applications, could provide power for generators and funfair attractions such as carousels.

The two forward gear Colonials were capable of rattling along a country road at 3.5mph. By modern standards this would be unacceptably slow. It should be remembered, however, that a heavy draught horse team would travel no faster and would require frequent rest breaks. The Colonial Class G, weighing 13.25 tons, had the ability to handle eight times the load that could be achieved by four English Shire horses on a hard, level surface.

In agricultural applications the 4-cylinder Marshall Classes D and F could replace twenty heavy draught horses. There was, however, a problem with the Marshall Colonials for British farmers. Even the Classes C and E, the 2-cylinder lightweights, weighed around 8 tons and proved too heavy for the soft, moist British arable soils. A Marshall Colonial bogging and sinking into the mud in 1910 would prove a nightmare for a farmer. Apart from another Colonial, it would have taken the resources of a steam traction engine to recover the big machine, with the always present risk of the recovery unit itself becoming bogged!

Previous page: A 1914 4-cylinder 70hp Marshall Colonial Class F. The big engine has dual ignition and two spark plugs per cylinder. It is of the 'square' design, having a bore and stroke of 6.25in. The four cylinders are water-cooled, utilising an enclosed circuit system with a radiator and fan. The example is therefore a rare tropical version, as the standard Colonials had an evaporative system and were equipped with a large capacity hopper which relied upon the thermal siphon principle for water circulation. This 12-ton tractor spent its working days hauling supplies along endless Australian outback trails to remote sheep stations and returning with wool to the railheads. Owned by Nev Morris.

The author at the controls of a 1911 Marshall Colonial 2-cylinder Class E. This classic tractor is preserved for posterity and is one of many historic icons on display at the Pioneer Settlement Village in Victoria, Australia. Note the open evaporative cooling system. *(Courtesy M Daw)*

It is not surprising therefore, that all but two of the Colonial tractors (this figure cannot be confirmed) produced were exported to Iran, India, Argentina, Canada, South Africa and Australia. The actual number of Colonials manufactured cannot be determined with certainty, but it is believed that over 100 units were sent to North America (principally Canada) and it is likely that between 300 and 400 units were produced in total, with a final batch being sent to Russia.

MARSHALL SINGLE CYLINDER DIESELS

During the late 1920s, Marshall's financial fortunes had declined to a dangerous level. The era of steam had all but gone and the mighty Colonials had become outdated and the design abandoned. But a growing number of farmers were becoming attracted to the new generation of Fordsons, Internationals and Fiats and saw them as the new technology in agricultural power farming.

A special advisory committee, set up by the Marshall board to re-energise the ailing firm, recommended that drawings for a new tractor be urgently prepared by the chief design engineer Samuel Dawson. It was noted that the German Lanz Bulldog was the top-selling European tractor. In great secrecy, a Lanz 15-30 was acquired and transported to the Gainsborough Works where it was dismantled and examined.

The horizontal, single-cylinder, valveless 2-stroke engine was of the semidiesel principle, with a compression ratio of only 4.5 to 1, and it was considered that Marshall should proceed with this type of basic design, which would keep tooling costs to a minimum. Significantly, however, Dawson decided that the Lanz concept could be improved upon by making the Marshall engine a full compression ignition diesel of 15.5 to 1 compression ratio.

In 1930 the Marshall 15-30 horizontal, single-cylinder diesel tractor was released. It featured an 8.0 x 10.5in bore and stroke and Marshall's own design of fuel injection equipment. In field conditions the Marshall 15-30 proved no match for its Lanz equivalent and the injection equipment was unacceptably troublesome. In 1931 the tractor was re-equipped with a Bosch fuel pump and injector, but still its performance was considered unsatisfactory and only a small number of 15-30s were produced. The few that had been sent to overseas agents were returned to the factory at

This excellent example of a Marshall 18-30 is part of an extensive collection of transport memorabilia owned by Sandstone Estates of Centurian in South Africa. It is one of the few remaining 18-30 Marshall tractors in existence. *(Courtesy Sandstone Estates Pty Ltd)*

SEMIDIESEL LANZ OR FULL DIESEL MARSHALL?

The semidiesel Lanz type engine had a compression ratio of around 5 to 1 compared with the Marshall full diesel 15.625 to 1. This meant that the pressures exerted throughout the Marshall engine (including cylinder wall, piston, big end bearing, gudgeon and crankshaft) were very much greater than those exerted in the Lanz. However, the lower pressures and compression of the Lanz resulted in it being unable to entirely burn all its fuel. The unburned fuel, although messy in the exhaust system, provided additional lubrication for the cylinder wall. The Marshall, being full diesel and providing it was operating at the correct temperature, did not, in theory, have this bonus lubrication.

Another point in favour of the Lanz system was that, as the piston rings and cylinder wall experienced normal wear, the resultant loss in compression pressure made no appreciable difference to its performance. Similar wear in the Marshall (which would occur more rapidly for reasons already outlined) would have a more detrimental effect on performance.

As a consequence the Lanz, together with other similar semidiesel tractors, enjoyed a reputation of being more durable and less prone to fatigue failures than the Marshall. (Marshall enthusiasts will not appreciate these comments, as there is much friendly rivalry between followers of the two tractors. In no way is it being suggested that the Marshall was prone to structural weakness or that it suffered from early engine deterioration.)

The big advantage with a Marshall was that the tractor could be started without a blowlamp being needed to preheat the combustion area, as was required with a Lanz. A Marshall operator needed only to light and insert an igniter into the fitting in the cylinder head, activate the decompression valve and crank the engine into life. The postwar Field Marshall series incorporated a breach block, into which an explosive cartridge was fitted. The operator had merely to strike the cartridge with a hammer and the engine would start. (It is interesting to note that in 1926 the German-made Colo had a 3-cylinder, 30hp 4-stroke engine which was started by an explosive cartridge.)

Marshall's expense. This only served to worsen the company's already tenuous financial position.

The Marshall 18-30 was introduced in 1932 to replace the 15-30. Despite the company spending money it could ill afford on the development of the new model, the performance and reliability results showed only a slight improvement. The production of the 18-30 appears to have been discontinued in 1934, although the accuracy of this is hard to substantiate, as 18-30 tractors continued to be available until 1938. It is likely the final sales were drawn from unsold stocks that had been manufactured, although not necessarily assembled, prior to 1935. It is known, however, that there were only seventy-two Marshall single-cylinder tractors sold between 1930 and 1934.

The Marshall 12-20 arrived on the scene in 1935 and proved to be the first of the Marshall single-cylinders worthy of the name. This was an all-new tractor with the cooling radiator cells mounted crossways above the cylinder block. The bore and stroke had been reduced to 6.5 x 9in and was to remain as such for all future single-cylinder Marshall diesel tractors. Apart from the first few produced, which were provided with only two forward gears, the new model had three well-spaced forward gears, albeit

A 1936 Marshall 12-20 restored by the author. It is equipped with full-width mudguards, a feature of 12-20 tractors exported to Australia. The 12-20 was produced from 1935 until 1938, during which a total of only 212 were made.

Rear view of the author's Marshall 12-20. The majority of 12-20 units produced were painted green with red wheels, however individual tractors could be ordered directly from the factory painted in any colour selected by the buyer.

with a somewhat high reverse gear. A cone clutch was located on the left side end of the crankshaft, encased within the belt pulley.

The 12-20 was followed in 1938 by the Model M. Only minor changes were introduced, including a maximum rpm increase from 680 to 700, bearings instead of bushes in the front axle and the option of a winch, lighting gear and canopy.

Both the 12-20 and the M proved to be dependable and solid performers, well capable of out-pulling the Fordson N, which was Marshall's main competitor in Britain. The M was produced in limited numbers throughout the war years until 1945 when it was replaced by a new generation of Marshall tractors featuring a more modern appearance and now known as Field Marshalls.

FIELD MARSHALLS

Field Marshalls were produced from 1945 until 1957. The Series 1, and later the Series 2, had three forward gears. The Series 3, released in 1949, featured a dual range, six forward speed transmission, as did the final model, the Series 3A, which was released in 1952. The Series 3 and 3A also featured a centrally mounted pto shaft, as distinct from the offset pto shaft of the previous models.

It is estimated that between 1945 and 1957 approximately 10 000 Field Marshalls were produced. In addition to British sales they were exported to numerous countries including the West Indies, Algeria, Spain, Zimbabwe, Australia, New Zealand, Jamaica, Canada, France, Portugal, Tanzania and South Africa, where they attracted a relatively small but dedicated following.

Grain farmer Pat O'Brien regularly uses his Field Marshall Series 3A for cultivating, even although he also has a stable of modern tractors. None, however, have the operating economy of this single-cylinder classic, which on this type of application consumes only one gallon of diesel fuel each hour.

An interesting photo taken at the Antique Society's Leduc show, Alberta, Canada, of a Field Marshall Series 3A owned by Stan Kick (seated). The tractor is supplying power to a machine (not shown) via a flat belt driven by the tractor's belt pulley. The 3A was the last of the Field Marshall series and the only model to be painted orange. *(Courtesy J Kick)*

MARSHALL MP6

Between 1956 and 1961 Marshall manufactured a truly outstanding heavyweight tractor named the MP6. The Field Marshalls had been discontinued as it was obvious the single-cylinder technology had run its course. Competition from tractors such as the David Brown 50D, Fordson Power Major, Massey Harris 745D, Chamberlain Champion and the Cockshutt 50D had convinced Marshall to produce an all-new heavyweight wheeled tractor.

A Marshall MP6. The reference to the 'Marshall 70' decal on the bonnet is a carry-over from the 1955 prototype which was originally known by that name. By way of interest, this was followed by the unsuccessful MP4 prototype, powered by a Meadows 4-cylinder engine, which did not enter production. Owned by Jesse Martin.

The big broadacre MP6 was powered by a 6-cylinder, 350cu in Leyland diesel engine, which developed 68.6 belt hp, resulting in an impressive drawbar pull of 10 800lbs at 1.35mph. The weight of the tractor, including water ballasted tyres, was 6.2 tons. Six forward and two reverse gears provided an excellent working range.

Unlike the single-cylinder Marshall, which was tedious to operate owing to constant vibration and staccato exhaust note, the MP6 was a delight to drive. The comfortable upholstered seat was offset to the right to facilitate easy following of a furrow. The gearshift, mounted on a pedestal, fell conveniently to the operator's left side. A large platform provided ample room for stretching legs and even standing, to ease cramped muscles during a long period at the controls.

In its home country of Britain, the Marshall MP6 proved to be virtually unsaleable. This was not on account of any design or technical inadequacies, but simply because in 1956 British farmers were not ready for a 6-ton tractor and there were few implements available which could have done justice to the tractor's pulling capacity.

Accordingly, of the 200 MP6 tractors produced, only ten were sold in Britain and the remaining 190 were exported to established overseas Marshall agents. From a total of thirty-three tractors sent to Australia, twenty-one were purchased by Western Australian grain farmers. French agent SEDIM imported thirty-six of the tractors, and Cory Brothers imported thirty-three for their outlets in Spain, Portugal and Algeria. Another major importer was the West Indies Sugar Company, which took delivery of twenty-five tractors.

Production of the MP6 was discontinued prematurely in 1961, due to a complex sequence of marketing and financial implications. This effectively brought the era of the Marshall classics to a close.

This rear view of the Marshall MP6 shows the roomy platform and the offset upholstered seat. In the 1950s this would have been considered unusually comfortable and well appointed.

Orenstein & Koppel S32K

In modern times the giant German conglomeration Orenstein & Koppel is recognised as a leading manufacturer of industrial equipment ranging from mammoth excavators to shopping centre escalators. Few people are aware that its origins can be traced back to 1876, when engineers Benno Orenstein and Arthur Koppel formed a business relationship and opened a small metal fabricating workshop in Berlin.

The business rapidly expanded, eventually embracing a diversity of heavy engineering products. In 1938 the first Orenstein & Koppel tractors were introduced, powered by the company's own advanced and extremely robust 15hp single-cylinder and 30hp 2-cylinder full compression ignition diesel engines. The two engines shared the common bore and stroke of 115 x 170mm.

In 1941 a German-assembled side valve Ford petrol engine was used in a special Orenstein & Koppel industrial tractor which was equipped with an on-board industrial generator. Both this and two additional generator tractor models were used for military purposes during World War II.

After halting production during World War II, O&K recommenced making agricultural trctors in Berlin in 1949. It appears the O&K factory was one of the first engineering works in Berlin to recover from the destruction of the war. However the production of tractors was transferred the following year to a new facility at Dortmund.

The postwar Orenstein & Koppel tractor engines again featured a standardised cylinder bore and stroke dimension, this time of 115 x 160mm, in either a single or vee twin configuration. Maximum engine revolutions varied between 1400 and 1850rpm, thus enabling the company to offer engines with a power range varying from 16 to 36hp. In 1953 a 4-cylinder, 75hp version was introduced, still retaining the standardised cylinder dimensions.

The most unusual (and now considered the most rare) O&K tractor in the range was the 36-PS-Diesel-Kompressor-Schlepper-S32K, known simply as the S32K. Produced in 1951, this model was a comprehensively equipped, multipurpose tractor which was based on the agricultural S32A. The production run for the S32K, it is believed, was limited to around 100 units.

At the time the S32K was introduced, the German nation was still reeling from the effects of the war, and Berlin in particular remained in a shambles of devastation. This was despite the massive clean up and rebuilding program already well in progress. The S32K was actually custom-built to assist in the reconstruction of Berlin and was able to perform a variety of tasks.

Weighing 2.6 tons and with a transverse 2-cylinder vee configuration engine of 36hp, the tractor was well capable of performing normal agricultural applications. However the engine was also equipped with a clever adaptation which enabled the fuel supply to be cut off to the right side cylinder. The engine then remained running, being powered by the left side cylinder. The now driven piston in the right side cylinder displaced only air and served as an air compressor. The compressed air was first channelled to a cooler, mounted in front of the engine water radiator, then into a pressure tank built into the front of the right side mudguard.

The pressure in the tank was predetermined by an adjustable valve with a maximum setting of 120lbs per square inch (8.27 atmospheres). The single piston compressing the air was estimated to deliver around 100 cubic feet per minute. These figures indicate the unit could readily supply sufficient compressed air, at 1500 engine rpm, to operate a jack hammer. A dual outlet was provided for air hose couplings.

Mounted on top of the wide mudguards were an oxygen and acetylene cylinder. Gas hoses, plus welding and cutting torches, were stored inside the mudguards which doubled as lock-up storage cupboards.

Positioned below the tractor seat, and driven by a flat belt from the tractor's belt pulley, was a 5kW electric generator which supplied current for both remote lighting or power tools and also to an electric welder housed in the rear of the right-side mudguard. A power take-off, shaft-driven

Orenstein & Koppel S32K
Manufacturer: Orenstein & Koppel
Country of origin: Germany
Engine: O&K 16 V2
Type: vee twin diesel
Bore and stroke: 4.53 x 6.3in
Displacement: 202.8cu in
Rpm: 1500
Hp: 36 brake
Gears forward: 5
Gears reverse: 1
Weight: 2.6 tons
Front suspension: single transverse leaf spring
Starting method: provision in each cylinder for an igniter. A decompression valve is actuated during handcranking or using the optional electric starter motor.

Opposite page: An Orenstein & Koppel S32K in the author's collection. When obtained it was a rusted out hulk requiring a major restoration. The controls for converting the right side cylinder are visible. The air cooler is located in front of the radiator, behind the hinged front grill, and the inlet and outlet pipes can be clearly seen. The outlet pipe leads to the air pressure tank. The small door in the front of the mudguard gives access to the main pressure relief valve. The pressure gauge can be seen located on the side of the right mudguard and the two air outlets are positioned on top of the guard. Note the hinged lock-up compartments built into the mudguard sides.

A graphic taken from the original instruction manual, showing an S32K with its gas cylinders, electric generator and winch.

winch was located behind the differential housing. Rear sprags were fitted to anchor the tractor during winching operations.

There is no question that the Orenstein & Koppel S32K was indeed a versatile tractor. Amid the bombed out ruins of Berlin it could be used to operate a jack hammer to break up fallen masonry, weld or cut up distorted tram lines using an oxyacetylene gas flame, provide emergency power to hospitals or industry, winch down teetering destroyed buildings and, if not required for these tasks, plough up playing fields and parks to enable desperately required vegetables to be planted.

Orenstein & Koppel discontinued the production of tractors in the mid-1950s.

Rear view of the author's S32K. The belt pulley for driving the generator and the pto shaft for powering the winch are both evident.

The big semidiesels

O n a still night, under a frosty, starry sky, the sound of a big single-cylinder tractor carried for miles. It was a magical experience, just listening. Each tractor had its own individual, characteristic rhythmic thump. A farmer's wife could identify her husband's Bulldog, even though it was ploughing in the back paddock. Then there was Fred over on the other road on his Landini—he too was working late. In the opposite direction, Alfredo was obviously doing the night shift on his Breda crawler. It had a higher pitched thump, and if you listened carefully you could just hear the rattling of its crawler tracks. Alfredo's place was at least five miles away as the crow flies… Many older rural folk will be able to relate to such a scenario with a degree of nostalgia and personal recollection.

The big semidiesel tractors which emerged in the 1920s were uniquely European in origin. Only a very few were imported into North America, however some makes became familiar sights in far-off agricultural regions including China, Peru, India, South Africa and New Zealand. Australia in particular proved a fertile market for at least three makes of European semidiesel tractors, while two indigenous brands, modelled on their European counterparts, were also manufactured.

The great appeal of the single-cylinder semidiesel engines was their simplicity. With only three prime moving parts (i.e. piston, conrod and crankshaft) and maximum engine revolutions rarely exceeding 700rpm, these engines were practically indestructible. Their massive components were grossly overbuilt by modern standards, giving them an unparalleled reserve of rigidity and strength.

An additional endearment to farmers was the semidiesels' economy of operation. Being of low compression design (as distinct from full compression ignition diesel) they could be fuelled with a whole array of low volatility fluids, including peanut oil, discarded liquefied fat and sump oil drained from other engines. But the most common fuel used was a crude naphtha or mineral oil, similar to marine bunker oil. Such fuels could be purchased for a fraction of the price of petrol, kerosene and even refined diesel. Further, the quantity of fuel consumed, based on a

per hp hour calculation, was generally half that of a similar capacity tractor having a conventional multicylinder engine.

Internal engine pressures of the semidiesels were significantly lower than experienced in full diesel engines. This was another bonus feature, as stresses on components, including seals and gaskets, were considerably reduced.

Certainly, driving a semidiesel created a constant assault upon the eardrums. Then there was the acid rain. Commonly emitted from the chimney stack, acid rain enveloped both tractor and operator, and became particularly obvious by the end of a long shift. The very nature of the low compression engine prevented a total burning of all the fuel. The unburned fuel collected on the inside of the chimney and, even if cleaned out regularly, it was impossible to stop some of the sticky substance, black with carbon, from being ejected into the atmosphere.

The following table provides some revealing figures for a typical single-cylinder, semidiesel, valveless 2-stroke hot bulb engine compared with a 4-cylinder full diesel engine.

Item	1-cyl. semidiesel 2-stroke	4-cyl. diesel 4-stroke
Cylinder compression:	130lbs per sq. inch	500lbs per sq. inch
Fuel pump pressure:	150lbs per sq. inch	1200lbs per sq. inch
No. of injectors:	1	4
Distance travelled by piston at normal operating rpm:	16.89km in one hour	78.85km in one hour
No. of movements made by prime moving parts:	97 200 in one hour	1 287 000 in one hour

From their introduction in the 1920s, the big semidiesels gained a degree of refinement and sophistication over the next three decades. But by 1950 their days were numbered. Farmers had become disenchanted with their noise, vibration and tedious starting procedure involving preheating the hot bulb portion of the cylinder head with a blow lamp. Only Lanz persevered with design improvements to the Bulldogs, and in the 1950s they were given a new lease of life with the introduction of higher revving and increased compression engines, featuring a light alloy piston and new loop scavenging system. Engine vibration was reduced and an exclusive Lanz/Bosch electric starter motor fitted. But by 1960 even the Bulldogs were discontinued.

The following are examples of a few of the big semidiesels, each of which attracted, in its day, a following of enthusiastic farmers in scattered pockets around the world.

BREDA

The Italian firm of Soc. Italiana Ernesto Breda entered the tractor business in 1920 with a 4-cylinder, 30hp petrol-powered unit. It appeared to have been modelled upon the recently introduced Fiat 702 tractor. The Breda tractors failed to attract a significant following, despite the addition of variants of the original model.

In the 1930s a Breda crawler was added to the range, powered by a German Junkers 2-cylinder, 2-stroke engine. The Junkers engine featured a balancing piston, a design that was to appear years later in the British-made David Brown 2D tractors and Commer 'Knocker' trucks. The Australian firm of Jelbart also experimented with this type of balanced engine. However the Junkers-powered Breda did not prove reliable and the project was discontinued.

In 1948 Breda released the 50 SD crawler tractor, weighing in at 5400kg and powered by a single-cylinder semidiesel engine. This was followed a year later by the 6-cylinder 70 D crawler and in 1950 the 50 D was added to the crawler range. Apart from their engines, the 50 SD and the 50 D were nearly identical tractors (including the track gear).

A left-hand view of a 1949 Breda crawler. The tractor is in remarkably sound original condition. The track gear is identical to that fitted on later multicylinder Breda crawlers. Owned by John and Merna Payne. *(Courtesy J Payne)*

The 50 SD engine was a rugged horizontal, valveless 2-stroke hot bulb semidiesel of 12 litre capacity with a 9.252 x 11.023in bore and stroke. It achieved its 50hp at a thumping 600rpm. Common to this type of engine, it featured crankcase compression and dry sump lubrication. The engine drive was through a four plate, foot-operated clutch to the four forward and two reverse speed transmission. Steering was by two lever-controlled multiplate clutches plus drum brakes. The oscillating track suspension enabled the crawler tracks to gain good ground adhesion in all types of terrain. The drawbar pull of the 50 SD was 8000lbs at 1.55mph.

A right-hand view of the Breda 50 SD, which was its export model type (in Italy the tractor was known as the TC 50). This particular unit is serial No. 3867. The hand cranking wheel, used for starting the engine, is stored at the rear of the operator's seat. *(Courtesy J Payne)*

A schematic drawing of the Breda SD 50 which shows the engine, transmission and track drives in detail.

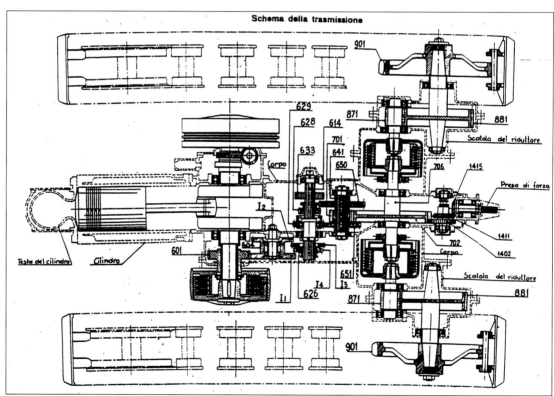

HSCS STEEL HORSE

In 1900 Clayton Shuttleworth Ltd, the distinguished manufacturer of steam engines and grain threshing machines, was persuaded by a group of wealthy Hungarians to take over control of a farm machinery works in Budapest, on a partnership basis. The Hungarians in the partnership were Matthius Hofherr and Jamos Schrantz. The new company was named Hofherr-Schrantz-Clayton-Shuttleworth. The name was eventually shortened to HSCS—no doubt to everyone's relief.

The HSCS threshing mills and steam engines produced in Budapest became widely known and held in high regard. But it was not until 1922, following some prototype experimentation with petrol engine tractors, that the company introduced its first semidiesel tractor, the HSCS Steel Horse. (My research suggests it is more than likely that the Lanz Bulldog design engineer Dr Fritz Huber contributed to the creation of the HSCS Steel Horse. There is no documented evidence of this, but it must be remembered that the majority of the Lanz files were destroyed during the World War II bombing attacks on Mannheim.)

Henrich Lanz AG had a close fraternity with HSCS dating back to the 1920s, culminating in 1938 when HSCS was experiencing serious financial hardships. During that year Lanz negotiated with the HSCS bankers and purchased the HSCS's assets. In view of this long-term association, the link between Dr Huber and the HSCS tractor is probable.

A diagram explaining the workings and simplicity of the HSCS engine.

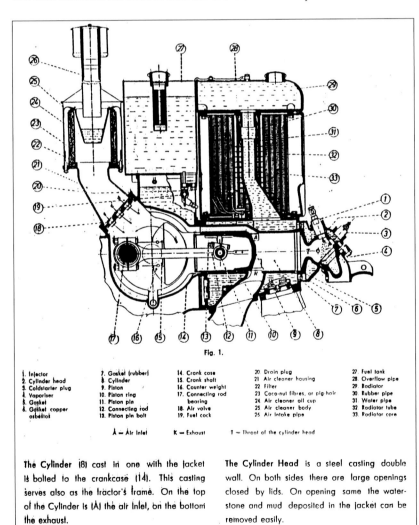

Fig. 1.

1. Injector	7. Gasket (rubber)	14. Crank case	20. Drain plug	27. Fuel tank
2. Cylinder head	8. Cylinder	15. Crank shaft	21. Air cleaner housing	28. Overflow pipe
3. Coldstarter plug	9. Piston	16. Counter weight	22. Filter	29. Radiator
4. Vaporiser	10. Piston ring	17. Connecting rod bearing	23. Coco-nut fibres, or pig-hair	30. Rubber pipe
5. Gasket	11. Piston pin	18. Air valve	24. Air cleaner oil cup	31. Water pipe
6. Gasket copper asbestos	12. Connecting rod	19. Fuel cock	25. Air cleaner body	32. Radiator tube
	13. Piston pin bolt		26. Air intake pipe	33. Radiator core

A — Air Inlet   K — Exhaust   T — Throat of the cylinder head

The Cylinder (8) cast in one with the jacket is bolted to the crankcase (14). This casting serves also as the tractor's frame. On the top of the Cylinder is (A) the air inlet, on the bottom the exhaust.

The Cylinder Head is a steel casting double wall. On both sides there are large openings closed by lids. On opening some the water-stone and mud deposited in the jacket can be removed easily.

All HSCS tractors had great character (which endears them to present-day collectors) but none more so than the L25 crawler produced in 1937. The sole purpose of the steering wheel and shaft, carried at the rear of the tractor, was for inserting into the end of the crankshaft. This enabled the operator to rock the flywheel in a pendulum motion in order to start the engine, following the heating of the hot bulb portion of the cylinder head with a blow lamp. This interesting 25hp HSCS L25, serial No. 5571, is on display at the Booleroo Steam and Traction Preservation Society's museum in South Australia. Its owner and restorer is Ferg Innes.

The 1950 G35 was one of the final production models of the HSCS single-cylinder tractors. The Budapest factory was taken over by the Communist government and the name changed to Red Star Tractors. Later it was changed again, this time to Dutra, and a whole new model range was introduced. This example of an HSCS G35 has been restored by Warren and Rodney Kemp.

CRUDE OIL TRACTOR

With economy as its keynote — this ruggedly built, money saving power unit is the eagerly awaited answer to all farming needs. Here is the most amazing and thoroughly efficient tractor on the market — and one that requires the least looking after. The Secret? — Here it is in a nutshell. The Steel Horse Tractor is a single cylinder 2-stroke crude oil burner of the most reliable design yet developed. Dispensing entirely with spark plugs, carburettors, valves and other troublesome parts, this outstanding tractor cuts wear, mechanical faults and fuel consumption to an absolute minimum. A special vaporiser and injector ensures the utmost smoothness of running, whilst lower engine R.P.Ms. afford sturdier power with a longer trouble free life.

On every job — from every point of view "Steel Horse" saves its cost and keeps on saving. It is the ideal tractor for the man on the land.

NOW AVAILABLE

Full details and specifications of Steel Horse Tractors are available in an interesting coloured Booklet. Call or write now for complete information.

BROWN & DUREAU LIMITED
Head Office: 422 Collins Street, Melbourne.

This advertisement for the HSCS R30-35 appeared in the Australian publication the *Leader*, May 1950.

These photos show the author demonstrating the starting procedure for an unrestored KL Bulldog. *(Courtesy M Daw)*

1. Originally the hot bulb portion of the cylinder head would have been heated with a blowlamp. In the interests of convenience and safety, most collectors of semidiesel hot bulb tractors now utilise gas for the preheating process.

2. Whilst the hot bulb is warming up, the tractor is greased and lubricated. This photo shows the lubricating pump being turned by hand, resulting in all internal engine components getting a liberal coating of oil prior to starting.

3. The steering wheel and shaft is easily removed by simply pressing the release lever. It is then taken to the right side of the tractor and inserted into the end of the crankshaft.

4. By now the hot bulb will be glowing cherry red, the fuel primed and the engine ready for starting. It only remains for the operator to summon up the energy required for rotating the big flywheel fore and aft in a pendulum motion. With a cloud of smoke the big engine will burst into life, accompanied by a series of thumping detonations.

KL BULLDOG

Prior to the outbreak of World War II, the Australian company Kelly and Lewis (KL) was well established as the nation's leading importer and service agent for German Lanz Bulldog tractors. Following the cessation of hostilities in 1945, the Victorian State government encouraged KL to construct a new factory and foundry principally for producing an 'Australianised' Bulldog tractor. This was at a time when the world shortage of tractors coincided with Australia's desperate need to increase its farming acreage.

The German Lanz tractors were unprocurable in 1945, as the factory had been seriously damaged during the war. Accordingly, arrangements were made to produce the KL Bulldog as a direct copy of the Lanz D8506 (see page 135).

LANDINI

The Landini tractor ancestry can be traced back to 1884 when Giovanni Landini opened a workshop in the village of Fabbrico, located deep in the fertile Reggio Imilia farmlands of Northern Italy. In 1910 his fascination with internal combustion engines resulted in the creation of Italy's first single cylinder, semidiesel hot bulb engine.

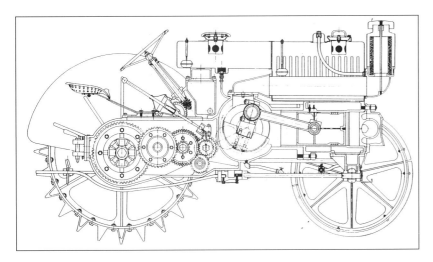

The 40hp 2-stroke Landini was hopper-cooled, relying on the thermo-siphon principle to circulate the coolant. The vertical container, shown located in front of the hopper, was the air intake filter, through which the air was drawn into the crankcase via a non-return valve. The air was then pressurised within the crankcase due to the movement of the piston returning on its power/exhaust stroke. The returning piston finally exposed a port, permitting the pressurised air in the crankcase to escape into the combustion chamber, where it was compressed and received an injection of fuel. The heated hot bulb caused the pressurised air/fuel mixture to detonate, thus providing the energy of the power stroke. *(Courtesy Landini)*

A Super Landini being re-fuelled whilst it is operating a threshing mill driven by a belt from the tractor's belt pulley; the tractor remained in operation during the refuelling process. The fuel used would have been low-octane crude naphtha oil and therefore, although the open container was close to the exhaust chimney outlet, would not have constituted a fire hazard. *(Courtesy Landini)*

Super Landini specifications

Engine type: 1-cyl. horizontal type 2-stroke semidiesel
Bore: 240mm
Stroke: 270mm
Capacity: 12.2 litre
Compression ratio: 6 to 1
Max. engine revs: 620rpm
Gears forward: 3
Gears reverse: 1
Weight: 3650kg

The L 25 was one of the new-look postwar Landini tractors. It was equipped with 3-point linkage and marketed as a general purpose tractor in direct competition with the new range of Fiat, Lanz and other postwar European tractors. It remained in production until 1956 by which time 6994 had been produced. Landini advertising was imaginative and colourful. In this classic advertisement for the L 25 a comparison is made with the old-fashioned way of farming which meant heavy toil for both beast and man, still practised in some districts of rural Italy in the 1950s. *(Courtesy Landini)*

The Cv 55-60 (together with its smaller stablemate the Cv 35-40) was offered with an optional half-track configuration. This served as a compromise between the regular wheeled and full crawler units. The half track equipment was designed by the British company Roadless of Hounslow. Roadless half tracks were also available fitted to Massey Harris, Allis Chalmers, Fordson and some other tractors. Very few of the Landini–Roadless tractors were in fact sold. It appeared that European farmers, and in particular Italians, if contemplating a crawler, preferred to purchase the full track version. *(Courtesy Landini)*

The Landini Bufalo was added to the range in 1941. With 220 x 240mm bore and stroke and a 9.118L capacity, the engine produced 40 belt hp at 720rpm. It had four forward and one reverse gear and weighed 2800kg. When production of the Bufalo was terminated in 1950, only 160 (plus five prototypes) had been made. Consequently there are few examples remaining today and these are much in demand by collectors. Pictured above is a Bufalo retained for posterity in the foyer of the Landini factory.

Landini's premature death in 1924 deprived him the opportunity to witness, in the following year, the first of what was to prove a long lineage of Landini tractors emerging from the Fabbrico factory. The new tractor was powered by a Landini designed semidiesel 2-stroke engine, which was valveless, hopper-cooled and developed 30hp at 500rpm. The second model of Landini was a 40hp version introduced in 1932, which remained in production until 1937. A total of 1242 were manufactured during this period.

The largest capacity tractor in the Landini stable of the 1930s was the Super Landini, released in 1934. With modifications, this 12.2L tractor remained in production until 1951, by which time 3232 had been manufactured.

The Landini Cv 55-60 was the largest and the final single-cylinder, hot bulb tractor produced by the company. It entered the market in 1954 and its production ended in 1956, with only 449 units made. The short manufacturing run was due to the fact that by the mid-1950s the era of the big semidiesels was coming to a close.

Within the next few years Landini would unveil a totally new range of tractors with full compression ignition diesel engines. This was to be followed by the introduction of Perkins diesels and an association with Massey Ferguson.

In 1954 it was apparent to the Landini management that there was an increasing demand for crawler tractors, particularly in the more mountainous regions of Northern Italy. The company consequently instructed its design team to fast-track a new line of Landini crawlers.

LANZ BULLDOG

Of all the big semidiesels, the most widely known around the world was the Lanz Bulldog, manufactured at Mannheim by the long-established German company Henrich Lanz AG. Lanz tractors had been produced since 1912, but it was not until 1921 that the brilliant Dr Fritz Huber and his design team unveiled the first Bulldog HL. Unlike the earlier Lanz tractors with their multicylinder engines, the Bulldog was outstandingly simplistic in its concept. The 12hp engine consisted of one cylinder, one connecting rod and a crankshaft—and basically that was it! There were no valves, push rods, carburettor or electrics. The basic hopper-cooling meant that there was no radiator, water pump or hoses. The Bulldog could be fuelled on any combustible fluid of low volatility. It started readily after preheating the hot bulb portion of the cylinder head with a blowlamp and, very importantly, an unskilled farm labourer could carry out all maintenance and service.

Opposite page: Belt work was an important role for tractors in the 1920s, particularly those used in Europe. This Lanz archival promotional leaflet exemplifies the versatility of the original Bulldog to perform belt pulley operations. *(Courtesy Lanz archives, Mannheim)*

Exhibiting considerable foresight and innovation, Dr Huber broke new ground in European tractor evolution when in 1925 he introduced the 15hp Allrad Acker Bulldog. Remarkably, the tractor had 4-wheel drive and an articulated frame, features which were rediscovered by tractor designers in the 1960s. It was, however, ahead of its time and deviated from the Bulldog principle of simplicity, and most farmers were put off by its complexity. This photo was taken in the staff dining room of J Deere Works, Mannheim, the site of the original Lanz factory.

There was always a demand for road or 'transport' tractors in Europe. These were employed in a variety of applications, both industrial and agricultural. The agricultural versions were often used for hauling several trailers coupled together, loaded with farm produce, to provincial market centres. Such tractors differed from their straight agricultural counterparts by having sprung front suspensions and either open or enclosed truck-style cabs. Other additions such as lighting equipment, high road gear and highway tyres were also available. Illustrated is a 1939 55hp Bulldog, fully furnished for road work. *(Courtesy Lanz/J Deere archives)*

„BULLDOG" zieht einen Dreschsatz zur Arbeitsstätte.

„BULLDOG" treibt eine Lanz-Schrotmühle.

„BULLDOG" treibt eine Bandsäge.

„BULLDOG" treibt eine provisorisch aufgestellte Dynamo.

„BULLDOG" treibt einen Koksbrecher.

„BULLDOG" treibt einen Steinbrecher.

BULLDOG
wird eisenbereift oder
gummibereift geliefert.

———

BULLDOG
dient dem Antrieb
von elektrischen Ma-
schinen für die Er-
zeugung von Licht.

„BULLDOG" zieht einen Steinbrecher.

BULLDOG
wird auch als ortsfeste
(stationäre) Maschine
geliefert.

BULLDOG
mit Vierradantrieb u.
Greifern auf Vorder-
und Hinterrädern ist
der ideale Pflugmotor.

DSE 3
324 250.00

The 45hp Bulldog HR 8 (Model P) was one of the most successful in the Lanz range and sold widely around the world. This particular 1950 Model P has served its time in tropical Queensland, Australia, working in sorghum and wheat crops. The owner, Pat O'Brien, continues to use his tractor regularly; he finds the cost of the Bulldog fuel consumption to be less than half that of any of his modern tractors.

A 1956 photo of the author ploughing virgin country with a 2-furrow mouldboard plough mounted behind one of the new generation Lanz Bulldog D2416 (Model H). The demonstration proved the 24hp Bulldog had the drawbar pull capabilities equivalent to a multicylinder tractor of double the horsepower. *(Courtesy L Simon)*

The Bulldog HL was an instant success. Farmers who had been hesitant or unable to afford a tractor eagerly placed an order for the low-priced Bulldog. A long line of Bulldogs followed, all constructed on the same semidiesel hot bulb principle. Crawler, half track and row crop versions were introduced.

In 1951 Lanz unveiled a redesigned semidiesel engine which eliminated the necessity of a hot bulb and the blowlamp heating procedures. The new engine had a light alloy piston and was fitted with a unique Lanz/Bosch electric pendulum starter motor.

Deere & Co. of Moline, USA, progressively acquired a controlling interest in Henrich Lanz AG during the latter half of the 1950s. By that time over 200 000 Bulldogs had been built. In 1960 production of the Mannheim plant was switched to multicylinder John Deere tractors. The legendary Bulldog was relegated to history.

A cutaway view of the engine fitted to the Lanz Bulldog D2416. Note the flat headed alloy piston which replaced the heavy cast steel contour-headed piston of the earlier hot bulb Bulldogs. A Bosch pendulum starter motor engaged a starter ring on the flywheel and rocked the piston back and forth, but did not turn it over compression unless the engine had commenced to fire.
(Courtesy J Deere)

And here it is, the famous indestructible Bulldog Diesel engine supplying abundant power at fractional cost.

Only a short time ago it was beyond the fondest dreams of Diesel engineers to build an engine as efficient as this one, yet so remarkably uncomplicated and robust. The Bulldog has the high performance and flexible power of two-cycle design. Torque remains remarkably high, even at low engine speeds, and fuel consumption is LOWER than on any other tractor on the market. — Wear is negligeable in this powerful one-cylinder diesel engine for there are only a handful of moving parts and each is made of selected materials.

MCDONALD

Alfred Henry McDonald holds the distinction of being Australia's pioneer tractor producer. His first tractor, made in 1908, was the McDonald EA, powered by a 2-cylinder, petrol-fuelled 20hp engine of his own design. McDonald tractors were well suited to the hot Australian summers and performed more reliably than some of the imported competitor brands. A variety of models were produced, and in the 1920s the company imported both the twin-cylinder semidiesel Avance from Sweden and the Emerson Brantingham from the USA.

In 1929 the McDonald TX Super Diesel was introduced and took the place of the imported units. The TX could not be called a totally indigenous tractor, as was the case with the earlier McDonalds; the engine was based upon the Lanz 15-30 and the transmission was purchased from the American tractor manufacturer Advance Rumely Thresher Company.

A revised version of the first McDonald TX was the 36hp TWB, introduced in 1931. Its single-cylinder engine had a 9.25 x 10in bore and stroke, which remained standard measurements with all McDonald single-cylinder semidiesel tractors. Pictured is a restored 1936 example owned by Vic Muscat (standing at the rear). It is being driven by the celebrated Neal McDonald, son of the McDonald company's founder and highly decorated RAAF World War II fighter pilot who flew Bristol Beaufighters against the Japanese in the Pacific.

The engine lay horizontally and faced forward, in accordance with the Lanz design. But in the McDonald frame, the weight on the front axle was excessive. The tractor was nearly impossible to steer and there was insufficient weight over the driving wheels to obtain adequate traction. It was a case of back to the drawing board for the McDonald engineers.

The solution of the weight problem proved simple. The engine was rotated so that the cylinder head faced to the rear and the entire unit repositioned rearwards, thus transferring the weight to the driving wheels. Production of the redesigned tractor went ahead.

The view forward taken from the rear of the operator's platform of a McDonald TWB. The photo shows the hot bulb portion of the cylinder head being heated by a gas flame, necessary prior to being able to start the engine.

The McDonald single-cylinder crude oil tractors proved to be massively strong. Accordingly, they were used extensively in converting inhospitable country into grain fields. The undergrowth and root systems found in such areas were notorious for breaking ploughs and indeed occasionally broke tractors in half. Special 'stump jump' ploughs were specifically designed for this type of punishing work. There is no record of a McDonald tractor experiencing structural failures whilst engaged in developing this rough country.

Of course not every farmer required a tractor as big and rugged as a McDonald. Their sales were only minuscule when compared with the volume being obtained by International Harvester, Fordson or Massey Harris. In an endeavour to increase market penetration, McDonald offered farmers the company's own time-payment arrangements. During the mid-1930s farmers were still reeling from the financial implications of the Great Depression. Drought and floods were also not uncommon elements which affected an Australian farmer's income. These factors created some anxious moments for McDonald and its bankers, as some farmers were obliged to default with their time-payments. But the company managed to keep afloat under the shrewd guidance of its founder AH McDonald.

Like all semidiesel 2-stroke engines, swinging a McDonald into life could result in the engine running in reverse cycle. There was nothing to prevent it from doing so. An inattentive McDonald operator, unaware that the newly started engine was running in reverse, would be in for a shock. Upon engaging reverse gear to back out of the shed, they would quickly discover the result of his lack of attention when the tractor headed forwards, possibly with disastrous results. (Any classic tractor enthusiast wishing to learn more about McDonald tractors, road rollers, engines, etc. should acquire a copy of the book *AH McDonald, industrial pioneer*, (1995, ISBN 0 7316 4939 7). This, in my opinion, ranks as one of the great tractor books and was written by Neal McDonald, the son of AH McDonald, who had access to the entire collection of documents and photographs held within the company's archives.)

LANZ BULLDOG COPIES

During and immediately following World War II, the disruption to the flow of Lanz tractors and their spare parts proved a major problem to established foreign Lanz importers. As mentioned, the Australian company Kelly and Lewis manufactured a copy, the KL Bulldog, to get around this problem.

The Lanz agent in Argentina, Pampa Industria Argentina, was faced with a similar problem to its Australian counterpart. South America had been a fertile market for Bulldogs, particularly Argentina, Brazil, Bolivia and Peru. Government ministers encouraged the Argentinean importer to commence the manufacture of Bulldog tractors and parts. The model selected for local production was the popular 45hp HR8. It was decided it should be named the Pampa Bulldog.

In distant Germany, the Lanz factory was being speedily reconstructed after the war and new models devised. Completely involved with their own problems, the Lanz engineers had only scant knowledge of the events taking place in Argentina until they received an urgent cable requesting immediate assistance. Apparently the Pampa Bulldogs were suffering an epidemic of transmission failures. This was occurring despite the fact that all the gears and shafts were allegedly made to authentic Lanz blueprints.

The problems were ultimately solved by sending genuine Lanz gears to the Pampa factory. It was apparent that one or more of the local gears had been made with an in-built inaccuracy.

Yet another outright copy of the German Bulldog was the Polish Ursus, which appeared immediately following World War II. Prior to and during the war, under strict orders from the German military, Lanz established a number of branch service depots in Eastern Europe. These were primarily intended to provide parts and service for the Lanz tractors employed by the Wehrmacht, but also to assist with fitting gas producers to Bulldogs being used by farmers at a time of acute fuel shortages.

In the late 1940s the Communist occupying forces in Poland relocated these Lanz depots, together with many of their personnel, to Warsaw under the control of the State-owned Zaklady Mechaniczne Ursus SA. In due course a new tractor factory was established in the neighbouring town of Czechowice and production of Ursus Bulldogs commenced, using the technical expertise and blueprints confiscated from the original Lanz depots.

Other manufacturers of single-cylinder semidiesel tractors include: Percheron and Vierzon in France; Baumi, Deutz, Mais and Werwolf in Germany; Bubba, Degonello and Orsi in Italy; and Mavag and Robuste in Hungary.

The single-cylinder, 2-stroke semidiesel tractors had a depth of character all their own. Perhaps it is not so remarkable, after all, that they endured for so many years and frequently outsold their more user-friendly and sophisticated multicylinder competitors.

The single-cylinder Marshall and Fowler tractors from Britain have not been included in this chapter owing to the fact that they do not actually fall into the category of semidiesels; they were full compression ignition diesels, without the necessity for a hot bulb. The Avance and other Scandinavian hot bulb tractors are also not included, as they had twin cylinders placed vertically and had totally different characteristics and sounds to the single-cylinder engines.

The Ursus Bulldogs are in high demand by European classic tractor collectors. This picture is taken from Ursus promotional material. *(Courtesy D Posthuma)*

This photo of a 1955 Pampa, owned by the Van de Vyver brothers of Holland, has been kindly made available by Jan Egelmeers, a prominent European vintage tractor authority. *(Courtesy J Egelmeers)*

The BMC Mini,
a brilliant tractor—nearly

Classic tractor collectors fortunate enough to own an example of the attractive orange coloured BMC Mini become accustomed to being accused by less informed collectors of either having painted a grey Fergy orange or having not painted the BMC blue. Neither indictment has any validity, however one can sympathise with the accuser because it is a relatively unknown fact that the tractor was in fact designed by Harry Ferguson and, following a false start, the tractor was repowered and painted blue. Whilst not actually conforming to the classic tractor definition guidelines, the BMC Mini is very collectable and technically fascinating, therefore worthy of examination.

By 1960, the British Motor Corporation (BMC) was firmly established as a leading tractor manufacturer. Its range of Nuffield tractors sold strongly into the domestic market and also earned much-needed export income from sales around the world. However, it was evident to the BMC directors that, despite their successes, sales were being lost by not having a tractor to compete in the lightweight section of the market. The Ferguson TE series had been replaced by the more powerful 35 series and the BMC board felt this had left a marketing gap. Accordingly, it was decided to seize this perceived sales opportunity by creating a brand new tractor of around 20hp.

At that time, BMC not only produced Nuffield tractors but also Morris, Austin, Wolseley, MG and Riley cars plus a range of Morris Commercial and Austin vans and trucks. There was simply not the available capacity in the design department to rush through drawings for an all-new tractor.

Tractor magnate Harry Ferguson had severed his relationship with the Canadian-owned Massey Harris Ferguson in 1954. Among other projects, he had established Harry Ferguson Research Ltd for the purpose of furthering his interests in the development of 4-wheel drive transmissions and continuing his research into cutting edge tractor technology. BMC approached Ferguson with a request to design the proposed new lightweight

tractor. This was the sort of challenge Ferguson could not resist. It also presented an opportunity for him to engender a capital inflow to set against the costly work being carried out by his research team.

Although Harry Ferguson Research Ltd had a prototype tractor ready for field testing in under two years, BMC took a further three years to tool up for production. Consequently, the new BMC Mini was not released until 1965. Ironically, the tractor was by that time obsolete, in the sense that the niche volume market for a lightweight tractor had evaporated. British farmers now interpreted a lightweight tractor as one of around 40hp; they had been educated to the power advantages of the MF 135, the Fordson Super Dexta and the David Brown 880.

Despite its late arrival, the new orange-coloured tractor, with its cream wheels and radiator grill, not only looked good, it bristled with imaginative yet practical design features. Had its dimensions been 20 per cent greater, its weight 3000lbs instead of 2000lbs, and had it been powered by a 40bhp engine instead of a 15bhp unit, this tractor would undoubtedly have been a sales leader.

The engine chosen by BMC (obviously with the intention of keeping production costs down) was the massively successful 4-cylinder 948cc BMC A Series. More than 2 000 000 had powered Morris and Austin vehicles for over a decade. The engine was converted into a diesel unit by

BMC Mini-Tractor

noted diesel design engineer Harry Ricardo and given a rotary fuel pump and injectors. The compression ratio was increased to a high (even by diesel terms) 22.5 to 1. The Lanova indirect injection combustion principal was utilised and this, coupled with the high compression ratio, necessitated the liberal use of four glow plugs to start the engine on a cold morning. It was necessary for the battery to be in good condition and fully charged in order to cater for the amperage drainage created by the glow plugs. The Series A diesel engines were assembled at the BMC associate company Newage (Manchester) Ltd.

The fact remained, however—the little diesel lacked punch! The 38lbs feet of torque obtained at 1750rpm simply was not adequate even

With the bonnet folded forward, excellent access was provided for carrying out maintenance on the Mini. Note the belt-driven hydraulic pump mounted above the front of the engine. The hydraulic oil reservoir is located at the rear of the engine. The rocker cover would be familiar to owners of Morris Minor, Morris Mini, Austin A30 and Healey Sprite cars.

for a lightweight tractor. The engine revolutions fell away at the slightest suspicion of an increased engine load. The nine forward speed gearbox offset the disappointing performance of the engine to a degree. Indeed the three speed, four range constant mesh gearbox was a pleasure to use. Reverse and medium-range gear positions were opposite each other on the quadrant, resulting in a forward/reverse shuttle available in any of the gears, by simply notching the selector fore or aft.

An excellent feature of the Mini was the location of the 6½-gallon fuel tank. Traditionally, British lightweight tractors had the tank mounted over the engine, but the tank on the Mini was positioned below the operator's seat. This negated the problems of fuel spillage over the engine and the ensuing fire risk. Also, the centre of gravity was lowered, giving more stability to the tractor on steep country.

The hydraulic system was completely external. The pump, mounted above and in front of the engine, was driven by a vee belt from the crankshaft pulley. The hydraulic reservoir was placed in front of the instrument panel, whilst the cylinder and controls for the 3-point linkage were situated above the transmission housing. Servicing the hydraulic system could be achieved in a fraction of the time when compared with the traditional in-built system as favoured by most other tractor manufacturers.

The BMC Mini was provided with disc brakes. The two independent turning brake pedals could be isolated by swinging down a hinged third pedal, giving a safe, balanced brake control for road use. An easily reached, hand-operated latch locked the brakes when parking.

The rear, centrally located pto shaft could be operated in the 540rpm or 1000rpm mode. The 1000rpm speed was handy, not only for machinery designed to be operated at this speed, but it could also be used for operating light loads at 540rpm by simply idling the engine. This procedure resulted in significant fuel savings.

The Mini tractor was manufactured at BMC's Scottish plant at Bathgate. Not surprisingly, owing to the limited performance of the 948cc engine, the Mini was soon upgraded and renamed the Leyland 154. The profile remained the same but the big change was the replacement of the BMC A Series engine with the BMC B Series 1500cc unit. The new tractor was painted blue with silver highlights and, although never achieving the sales penetration of its rivals, became a common sight around dairy farms, orchards and wherever a utility tractor was required. This then is the reason why owners of a restored unfamiliar Mini tractor with its orange livery are frequently told that their tractor should have been painted blue!

A BMC Mini belonging to the author, on display at an agricultural show. Standing alongside is the author and seated is the tractor's original owner, Eric Atkins, who was reunited with his tractor, having parted with it fifteen years previously. *(Courtesy M Daw)*

T Herbert Morrell
and the Oliver Super 55

By the end of the 1940s, a clear pattern was emerging of what constituted the ideal general-purpose utility tractor. In Britain the market was dominated by Ferguson, David Brown and Fordson. Europe had new, innovative models from Deutz, Eicher, Fendt, Guldner, Kramer and numerous others. Across the Atlantic, North American farmers were turning in droves to the new Fords and Detroit-made Fergusons. Whilst still popular, the International Farmall A and Allis Chalmers B tractors were starting to show their age and no longer prevailed in the lower horsepower end of the market. In 1954 a new challenger surfaced—the Oliver Super 55.

In the 1950s, The Oliver Farm Equipment Company, with its headquarters at Charles City, Iowa, was a long established and highly accredited manufacturer of tractors. With such classics as the Oliver 70 and Oliver 90 having certified the company's tractor credentials back in the 1930s, any new Oliver model was welcomed with enthusiasm by farmers and gained considerable respect from the competition.

Oliver had a secret weapon in its arsenal in the guise of T Herbert Morrell. Morrell's professional qualifications included being a member of the Society of Automotive Engineers, and a Fellow (Distinguished Member) of the American Society of Agricultural Engineers. He joined Oliver in 1944 as a design engineer and was promoted to chief engineer in 1951.

T Herbert Morrell was to Oliver as Bert Benjamin had been to International Harvester. They were both men of the soil, having been born into the farming world and a much-loved but arduous lifestyle, frequently interrupted by natural disasters and inequitable financial returns. Therefore Morrell's motivation, when involved with a new model tractor design, was to make it as safe, reliable and functional as possible, within the parameters of pricing restraints. He *felt* for the farmer who would drive his creation. He wanted the tractor to be right.

One might imagine that Morrell's high principles would be standard among tractor designers. The reality

was that a few tractor design engineers were governed by production cost factors first and the welfare of the farmer second. This was perhaps understandable and did not, in the majority of cases, result in an inadequate tractor. But there are isolated examples, bordering on culpability, of tractor organisations rushing through untested designs and dumping inferior machines upon an unsuspecting farming community. Evidence of this was the necessity of establishing the Nebraska test facility for the purpose of determining the accuracy of manufacturer's claims.

T Herbert Morrell could not have achieved his integrity of design of the Fleetline range of Oliver tractors, introduced in 1947, without the full backing of Oliver's board of directors, who shared his aspirations. No tractor company could have tested its prototypes more thoroughly than Oliver, in an endeavour to produce a trouble-free tractor.

The design of the Oliver Super 55 was perhaps the most challenging for Oliver in the postwar years. In the USA, the highly successful Ford 9N/2N, with 306 221 sales to its credit, had been replaced in 1947 by the Ford 8N. A year later, in 1948, Harry Ferguson commenced the Detroit production of his TO 20. In that year International Harvester produced 20 825 Farmall A tractors and its derivatives. Allis Chalmers nearly equalled this total with 19 537 of its B/C series. It was

An Oliver Super 55 restored by the author.

clear to Morrell that to successfully break into this fiercely competitive segment of the market the Oliver design team had to come up with something really special.

When production models of the Oliver Super 55 were finally released in late 1954, it was obvious that this was a very special tractor. It was available with either a diesel or petrol engine, each with basically the same engine block. The dimensions of the Super 55 were similar to those of the recently released Ford NAA Jubilee and the yet to be released Ferguson TO 35. But the Oliver had unique features which guaranteed its instant appeal to the new generation of farmers who demanded a greater degree of comfort and sophistication in a new tractor.

This photo shows the 3-point linkage plus the heavy-duty swinging drawbar. Note the gear change lever located conveniently to the left of the operator's seat. The hydraulic control quadrant lever and the live pto shaft lever are on the right of the seat.

The diesel and petrol-powered Oliver Super 55 tractors were identical apart from their engines. These examples, both in the author's collection, show the petrol-powered unit in the foreground with the diesel in the rear.

The diesel and petrol Super 55 tractors were identical apart from the injection or ignition systems of their engines. The engine capacity was 144cu in and produced 35.88 belt hp in petrol form or 34.09 belt hp as a diesel. The drawbar pull of the diesel was 3641lbs at 1.43mph and only marginally greater than the petrol unit on account of its diesel torque advantage.

An unusual technical feature of the Super 55 was the dual ratio gearbox, with its silent running helical cut gears—including six forward and two reverse speeds—controlled by the conveniently located single side-positioned gearshift lever (a single shift lever was also used by Fiat with the dual-range gearbox in its 411 series, but unlike the clumsy gearshift of the Fiat, the Oliver slots were easy to select).

A live pto shaft, with an independent hand-operated clutch, was provided in addition to the foot-pedal-operated main engine clutch. This

The diesel engine of the Super 55. Note the Bosch rotary fuel pump and the neat arrangement of the diesel fuel lines.

modern feature enabled an operator to bring the tractor to a stop without interrupting the drive to the pto-operated implement.

The hydraulic 3-point linkage system was mounted within a separate compartment on top of the rear transmission housing, submerged within its own reservoir of straight lubricating oil. A constant running (live) 5 gallons per minute Vickers vane hydraulic pump, operating at 1500psi, provided an abundant flow and pressure resulting in a fast acting 3-point linkage with a 5000lbs lift at the cylinder. Interestingly, in order to avoid breaching any of Harry Ferguson's patents, Oliver collaborated with Vickers in designing hydraulic circuitry for the Super 55 that was able to provide draft and position control, which hitherto had been unique to the Ferguson System yet did not infringe the Ferguson patents.

In addition to the linkage for attaching mounted implements, there was also an excellent swinging drawbar, which extended well forward below the rear transmission housing. This provided safe towing or snigging with little chance of the tractor rearing.

In 1954 the majority of tractors were still equipped with drum brakes. The Oliver Super 55 was fitted with self-energising double-disc brakes. These were mounted within external housings on the differential shaft. This design gave much greater stopping power than conventional axle-mounted brakes. The disc brakes could be operated independently as turn assist brakes.

The positioning of the engine air intake under the bonnet, above and front of the radiator, resulted in less dirt being sucked into the oil bath air cleaner. The two sections of the radiator grill were easily removed, enabling foreign material to be cleaned from the radiator chaff screen.

It is interesting to review the technical features of the Super 55 and relate them to the British Ferguson TE or the American Ferguson TO

The petrol engine of the Super 55. The battery is located in a slide-out drawer for ease of maintenance.

series. The Fergusons were still in production during the first years of the Super 55. The 'little grey Fergy' was undoubtedly one of the most popular tractors ever, but in comparison to the Oliver it was antiquated. Or perhaps it would be more correct to state that the Oliver was a generation ahead of the Ferguson.

During this post-World War II period Allis Chalmers, Massey Harris, International Harvester, Case and John Deere all made successful takeover bids for European tractor companies. By so doing they were able to sell their tractors, sourced from their European factories, into 'soft currency' markets, including the British colonial countries where they gained a favourable monetary exchange and tariff advantages.

In an endeavour to establish a South Pacific facility, and noting that International Harvester had built a tractor factory in Australia, the Oliver management team researched the feasibility of building an assembly plant in that country. A Mr Les Dyke, representing Oliver, wrote to the Australian Prime Minister Ben Chifley on 7 September 1948, seeking an audience with him in either Sydney or Canberra. The stated objective was to discuss the part-manufacture of Oliver-wheeled tractors in Australia. Mr Dyke did not receive a reply from the Prime Minister until January 1949 which said in part '… I do not think anything would be gained by a discussion with me.' (I can only imagine that this negative comment was prompted by the fact that two local companies, Kelly and Lewis and Chamberlain Industries, had at that time each received government support to proceed with the construction of indigenous Australian tractors.)

Accordingly, owing to the lack of overseas Oliver manufacturing plants, it is believed that only a small percentage of the 44 070 Super 55 tractors produced were sold outside North America. For example, it is believed that only ten of these tractors were exported to Australia. This was largely due to global tariff barriers against the US dollar, which had the effect of restricting the export of goods made in the USA. Those Super 55s that were exported were often priced at nearly double that of the Ferguson TO and TE. Consequently—and despite the technological advantages built into it—this costing factor precluded the Super 55 from many markets outside the USA.

Only tractor people with an in-depth knowledge and experience of the Oliver Super 55 can appreciate just how good these tractors really were. The examples that have survived are a testimony to that great tractor designer, T Herbert Morrell. The Super 55 was replaced by the re-styled Oliver 550 in 1958.

The Alios Murr story

enjamin Holt, Meinrad Rumely and Giovanni Landini are but a few of the high-profile names linked inexorably to the century-old tractor industry. There are at least a score of others whose names have become familiar to anyone with even a passing interest in old tractors. But for each tractor megastar there have been countless tractor folk without whose toil and dedication there could not have been a tractor industry. They have embraced a diverse ambit of jobs, ranging from foundry workers to spare parts storemen, demonstrators to sales coordinators, field mechanics to accountants and design engineers to export managers. Plus, importantly, there were the local country dealers and their field representatives. Collectively, these folk constituted the anonymous mainstay of the tractor industry. Alios Murr was but one of these dedicated unsung heroes who, in his own quiet way, contributed significantly to the world of tractors.

BAVARIA

The old town of Traunstein is located north of the main Salzburg-to-Munich autobahn. A traveller pushing further north, through the picture-postcard Bavarian countryside, would eventually arrive at the tranquil village of Waging am See. It was here, in 1901, that Alios Murr was born.

To the west of Waging am See lies the town of Wasserburg am Inn, the birthplace of Dr Fritz Huber, who was born there in 1888. The destinies of Alios Murr and Dr Huber were to become implacably interwoven, with tractors being the common denominator.

Following his schooling at Waging, Alios Murr continued his search for knowledge at the University of Weihenstephan. In 1924 he obtained his degree in agriculture, then elected to study a further three years at the Ohm-Polytechnikum in Nuremberg, where he graduated in 1927 with an Honours Degree in Agricultural Engineering.

Murr's accomplishments and fascination with machinery were brought to the attention of Dr Fritz Huber, Senior Design Engineer of Heinrich Lanz AG

Mannheim. Huber invited Murr to join his team in furthering the development of the Bulldog tractor. The brainchild of Dr Huber, the Lanz Bulldog was receiving accolades throughout farming communities in Germany and beyond. This was the type of technology that intrigued Murr. The offer to join Lanz was too persuasive for him to decline, so in 1927 Alios Murr joined the Lanz team with Dr Huber as his mentor.

In order to gain field experience Murr was posted to the company's Munich branch where he served as supervising field engineer from 1928 to 1931. This proved a period of great contentment for him; he enjoyed the involvement with local dealers, service mechanics and farmers, plus the technical challenges which arose. An added bonus of being based in Munich was the opportunity to occasionally slip away for a few hours to visit his family in Waging.

Whilst out in the field, Murr was expected to telephone the Munich office each day in order to receive messages. On one occasion, during a quiet period in early 1931, he failed to check in—it appears the lure of a day's skiing

Previous page: Alios Murr (1901–1982). *(Courtesy Len Beechley)*

The tar fuel was heated in a reservoir located within the water jacket attached to the radiator casting, at the front of the tractor, above the hot bulb. As the temperature of the water rose the tar liquefied, enabling it to flow into the fuel pump and on to the atomiser. Note the special elongated hot bulb designed to produce the higher temperature necessary for the detonation of the tar fuel.

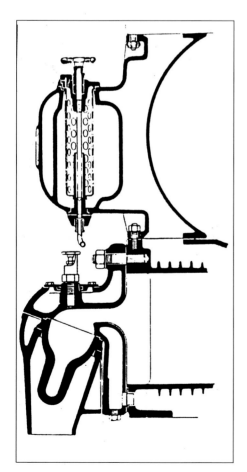

led him to temporarily change his priorities. The following day he was aghast to learn that Dr Huber had been urgently trying to contact him and instructions had been left that Murr should telephone him immediately upon his return.

Murr placed the call with some apprehension and, no doubt, a feeling of guilt, but was greatly relieved and elated to be told that he should immediately report back to Mannheim for a briefing, prior to being sent to Russia for several weeks.

RUSSIA

Russia had been a major buyer of Lanz steam engines up to the time of the revolution of 1917. Following the tumultuous after-effects of the Socialist takeover, Lanz exports to Russia declined considerably. In 1930, as part of an endeavour to stimulate business, Dr Huber had spent 10 weeks in the new Union of Soviet Socialist Republics supervising test procedures of Bulldogs specially modified for the severe Russian environment.

Upon Murr's return to Mannheim from Munich he was provided with a train ticket to the USSR and was briefed by Dr Huber on procedures for further analysing the results of the Russian tests. He was also to assist State-employed technicians, attached to collective farms, with the servicing of the Bulldogs.

His first destination in the USSR was a farm machinery test institute on the outskirts of Moscow. He then proceeded to Gigant, the centre of a vast collective farming area, where he arrived in mid-1931. The Bulldogs at the collective were being fuelled on low-grade naphtha and other crude oils, each having the consistency of tar. The tractors were modified Lanz 22-38 units which were first started on regular crude oil, using the blowlamp to preheat the hot bulb. The water in the cooling system was channelled to flow around a reservoir containing the tar fuel. As the water heated, it also heated the tar, softening and transforming it into a volatile fluid. The liquefied tar was then introduced into the combustion chamber, which incorporated a special elongated hot bulb designed to produce a higher than normal temperature of combustion.

Murr discovered that the tractors were only capable of producing around 20hp. He conducted experiments with a water injection device, which variably metered water into the hot tar, the quantity dependant on the governor setting. He found that this water injection worked reasonably efficiently and the power outlet of the engine increased to 35hp.

The region in which the collective farms were situated was adjacent to a tributary of the Volga River, and the Bulldogs were regularly driven across a sometimes submerged causeway which bisected the area. On one occasion, following torrential rain, the river had swollen and risen a full metre above the causeway. Undaunted, a Bulldog driver aimed for the opposite bank, but halfway across misjudged the width of the now hidden pavement. The Bulldog turned turtle and disappeared into 8 metres of water. The operator miraculously managed to scramble ashore, but his tractor was seemingly doomed.

Murr was summoned to the scene of the disaster. Physically fit and an expert swimmer, he dived down into the icy water and after several attempts succeeded in attaching a cable to the drawbar of the tractor which, he discovered, was lying inverted on the riverbed. Murr then recruited the nearby villagers and supervised the construction of a massive raft made from pine poles.

The following morning, a large manually operated winch was secured to the raft and half a dozen stalwart labourers applied their muscular powers to the levers. The tractor rose a few metres then the raft started to submerge. The crew jumped for their lives into the water. Minus its human cargo, the raft rose again until it reached a point of equilibrium just below the surface. The tractor remained hanging vertically, just clear of the riverbed. The raft was towed gently downstream using a rope connecting it to a tractor driven along the bank. Eventually the river bed shallowed to a gradual slope. The Bulldog settled onto its four wheels and was towed out of the river. According to Murr, the sole damage was a discharged battery. An hour spent changing the oils and fuel was all it took before the tractor was put back to work.

With winter approaching, Murr decided it was time to return to Germany. He believed his weeks spent in Russia had been productive in strengthening the ties between Lanz and the Soviet authorities.

Dr Fritz Huber.

The Bulldogs were frequently driven over a submerged causeway.

AUSTRALIA

On his return to Germany from Russia in the autumn of 1931, Murr spent the following year as a roving technical expert, devoting much of his time to directing technical training courses throughout the country. In late 1938, Dr Huber made arrangements for Murr to travel to Australia.

The original office copy of the letter sent to H Tronser by AL Bruns concerning the Lanz crawler problems, and which Tronser forwarded to Mannheim with a request that an experienced engineer be sent urgently to Australia.

```
                    Copy
                                        Melbourne - 23rd July 1938.

    H.Tronser Esq.,
    60 Hunter Street,
    SYDNEY - N.S.W.


    Dear Sir,

                    Re CRAWLER TRACTORS:

    We confirm the writer's conversation with you regarding  the failure
     of  model T crawler tractors in West Australia, where 15 tractors
    were imported in all; 14 direct from the factory and one which was
    sent from Melbourne.

    We have written our Manager  in Perth by to-day's airmail, requesting
    him to give us a separate and complete report on every crawler which
     he has in the West, even though they should not have been sold, but
      still new in stock. When this information is to hand we will pass
    it along to you, together with a separate report on each individual
    tractor supplied to clients and the troubles which have been expe-
    rienced with them.

    We understand that serious troubles have occurred with each tractor
    without exception, and this is the main reason that the writer indi-
    cated to you that he was very anxious you should make arrangements
    with the Lanz Co, to accept the return of all the crawlers from West
    Australia, including those which are new and also those which are broken.

    As you are aware, Lanz tractors have rather an unenviable reputation
    in West Australia, owing to the earlier mechanical difficulties ex-
    perienced there, and their present troubles with crawler tractors are
    likely to deal a death blow to possible LANZ tractor sales in this
    State.

    We feel that it is in the interests of the Lanz Co. as well as our-
    selves, that these crawlers should be removed from the State as early
    as possible and replaced, wherever possible, with wheel type machines.
    A certain amount of damage has already been done to future sales, but
    by special sales efforts we can, no doubt, overcome this.

    When making arrangements with the Lanz Co. for the return of these
    crawler tractors to Germany or elsewhere we would be glad to have
    confirmation that the Lanz Co. are prepared to accept responsibility
    for freight and other charges  incurred by us, importing these tractors
    into Australia, and also the responsibility for return freights.

    We assume, of course, that by application to the Customs Department
    we will be able to obtain refunds of duties paid on these machines,
    although it is possible that those that have been used and are now
    damaged, will not be subject to Customs refund.

    re QUEENSLAND REQUIREMENTS: We are not sure whether you propose to
    arrange for three of the unused crawlers to be shipped on to Queens-
    land, and would be glad to have your advice.

                                    Yours faithfully

                                    Geo.W.Kelly & Lewis Pty.Ltd.

                                    (Signed)  A. L. Bruns.
```

Hans Tronser, chief of Australian operations for Lanz, had forwarded a letter to Mannheim in July 1938 which he had received from AL Bruns, the managing director of the main Australian Lanz importer Kelly and Lewis (KL) Ltd. The letter was accompanied by an urgent request from Tronser that an experienced engineer be sent to Australia immediately, for

Page one of the letter sent by Lanz to the British Consulate General in 1938.

HEINRICH **LANZ** MANNHEIM
AKTIENGESELLSCHAFT

CTORS-THRESHERS-BALERS-HARVESTING MACHINERY

EXPORT-DEPARTMENT

To the British Consulate
General,

M ü n c h e n
Prannerstr. 11

BRITISH CONSULATE GENERAL
17 DEC 38
MUNICH

(Please quote)

YOUR REF.:	YOUR LETTER OF:	OUR REF.:	DATE:
		P 440 RFS/EK	16th Dec.,1938

Dear Sirs,

    May we ask you to kindly grant a Visa to

Mr. Alois **M u r r** , with Pass No. A 11 852

issued at   M u n i c h on 16/12/38.

    Mr. Murr is to visit Australia on our be -
half; he is expected to sail on January 8th, 1939 from
Naples on SS "Orcades" bound for Fremantle. A copy of
our to-day's letter dealing with the landing permission
in Australia, is attached.

    We should like to point out that for a num -
ber of years we have been doing a considerable amount
of business in Lanz Crude Oil Tractors throughout the
Commonwealth in co-operation with our distributors,
whose names and addresses are shown on the enclosure.
As a matter of fact, during the last eight years we
have delegated from time to time Representatives(Engi -
neers and Mechanics) to Australia.

    For the moment, we wish to delegate to that
country our Engineer Mr. Alois Murr. It will be his
job to visit our distributors for the purpose of study-
ing local conditions and to communicate some of his
wide experiences in our type of tractor to the techni -
can staff of our distributors.

    In view of the fadt that Mr. Murr is to visit
all our distributors and since his sojourn in the
various States of the Commonwealth of Australia will be
extended for a period of several weeks, or even months,
we will appreciate, if you will grant him a Visa for
at least 6 months.

- 2 -

the purpose of solving major problems that had arisen with the crawler Bulldogs as outlined in the KL letter. These problems were of such a serious nature, according to Bruns, that the future reputation of Lanz products in Australia was in jeopardy. In retrospect, there was undoubtedly a degree of over-dramatisation in the KL letter; Lanz wheeled tractors had established an irreversible record for strength and dependability throughout Australia that would take more than a few crawler problems to negate.

In due course a visa was obtained from the British Consulate General in Munich in December 1938 and Murr sailed for Australia on the SS *Orcades*, departing from Naples on 8 January 1939.

Tronser arranged for Alios Murr to visit widespread Australian farming regions and assist the various regional Lanz dealers to overcome the design irregularities of the crawler Bulldogs. Some customers and selling agents were insistent that Lanz take back their allegedly errant machines and refund all payments. Blueprints of redesigned components were airmailed to Murr, but not before several crawlers were returned to Tronser's care—the dealer in question being glad to offload the responsibility onto him.

Although it took several months and a considerable amount of travel, Murr eventually sorted out the crawler problems to the satisfaction of both farmers and dealers. Tronser cabled Huber to this effect and arrangements were made for Murr to return to Germany. It was already August and he was looking forward to spending the approaching ski season in his beloved Bavarian Alps.

On 3 September 1939 Britain and its colonies declared war on Germany. Alios Murr was shocked to find there would, therefore, be no opportunity to return to Germany in the foreseeable future. Bulldog imports from Germany abruptly ceased. KL seized the opportunity of gaining the services of an outstanding technician and offered Murr employment as a service mechanic, which he reluctantly but philosophically accepted.

When Japan attacked Pearl Harbor on 7 December 1941, the Australian Government quickly declared that, for their own protection, both German and Japanese nationals would be interned in special camps for the duration of the war. Thus on 22 February 1942 Alios Murr became internee No. 2157 at the Commonwealth Tatura Internment Camp, located in central Victoria. To Murr, this constituted a most graphic example of a person being in the wrong place at the wrong time.

Murr adopted a philosophical approach to his confinement. Life at the camp was relaxing and he spent much of his time delving into books. Meals were excellent and the guards became friends with whom he enjoyed a regular game of cards. Some letters arrived from his mother in Germany via the International Red Cross. He also received letters of encouragement and endearment from a young lady, Fay Forbes, whom he would eventually wed.

THE KL BULLDOG AFFAIR

Murr was released from Tatura on 22 May 1945 and re-employed by Kelly and Lewis. In far-off Mannheim, the Lanz works lay in ruins following a series of Allied bomb attacks during the final weeks of the war. Only the works' giant water tower, erected in 1900, remained intact.

Earlier, around 1944, the directors of KL had commenced important talks with the Australian government regarding the urgency of producing a local tractor for Australian farmers, to counter the worldwide shortage. These discussions resulted in licences being granted to KL for the purchase of steel and an inducement to built a new foundry in Tasmania. It was decided that the company would manufacture a copy of the Lanz 35hp Bulldog, to be known as the KL Bulldog. In 1945 it was announced that Alios Murr would supervise the development and construction of the new tractor.

In September 1945 Hans Tronser wrote a confidential note to Murr in which he expressed apprehension concerning the viability of the KL Bulldog project. Tronser had, in the meantime, accepted a position as an accountant to a Sydney company, pending the restructuring of Lanz. The KL directors were eager for him to accept a position with them as export manager, but Tronser had secret doubts about his ability to have an amicable work relationship with KL.

The association between KL and Murr became an unhappy one. Murr harboured a feeling of disloyalty to Lanz because of his association with the production of a Bulldog copy. Further, he experienced serious doubts about the integrity of the KL Bulldog blueprints. He argued with the board about what he described as ill-considered cost-cutting exercises.

Alios Murr standing beside his service van, pulled alongside a Lanz T crawler.

The board of KL Tractors Ltd advised the Australian government of its intention to produce 1000 tractors per year. In actual fact around only 900 were manufactured during the five-year production life. This advertisement appeared in mid-1948, despite the fact that the tractors did not become available for delivery until March 1949, owing to pre-production problems.

He cautioned, for example, that the piston surface thickness of ½in was blatantly inadequate when compared with the 1½in thickness of the Lanz piston surface. The crankshaft was not heat-treated and of insufficient diameter and strength to cater for the proposed 600rpm necessary to boost the power to 40hp. The fuel tank, he claimed, was too light in construction, but the board would only approve an increase from 18 to 14 gauge steel. Murr knew this niggardly approach would result in structural failures, as the light metal would be unable to withstand the vibrations of the engine.

By early 1946 his concerns regarding the KL project had come to a head. He stunned the KL board by tendering his resignation, thus leaving the program in disarray. He then applied to the National Security

Land Transport Department for permission to purchase a surplus army motor vehicle in order to commence his own business as a Lanz Bulldog repair technician.

Murr and his new wife Fay prospered in their new business. It was not long before they were able to purchase industrial premises in Melbourne and their enterprise expanded into the manufacture of Bulldog spare parts. Murr experienced a new freedom and contentment not matched since his early days in Bavaria. His name was held in high esteem by Bulldog owners throughout the nation, and he successfully commandeered the major share of Bulldog service work from Kelly and Lewis in his home State of Victoria.

What of the KL Bulldog? As a result of delays and frustrations, the tractor was not released until 1949. Despite the predicted production target of 1000 units per year, only 900 were manufactured during its five-year production life. The initial tractors were plagued with problems which included cracked pistons, broken crankshafts and leaking fuel tanks.

Hans Tronser did not join Kelly and Lewis but was appointed instead as managing director of the new Lanz (Australia) Pty Ltd and was responsible for the establishment of a sales and assembly branch in Sydney. The first of the technically sophisticated, new-look Bulldogs arrived from Germany in 1953, which immediately rendered the KL tractors unsaleable. In the 1960s Tronser returned to Mannheim where he was appointed to a senior executive position by the new incumbents, John Deere.

Alios Murr travelled to Germany with his wife in 1961 to visit his Bavarian birthplace of Waging am See. The historic Lanz organisation had been taken over in 1956 by US giant John Deere. Dr Fritz Huber had passed away on the 14 April 1942, his death perhaps hastened by the pressures from the Nazi Party to achieve the near-impossible task of producing a holzgas (gas burner) for his beloved Bulldogs. His nephew, Hansludwig Huber, worked in the old Mannheim factory as a design engineer, but now for John Deere.

Alios Murr worked in Australia until his retirement in 1981. He passed away peacefully in 1982. Although his name remains relatively unrecognised in the annals of tractor evolution, those who were privileged to know him recognise he was a significant and indeed unique cog in the vast realm of the world of tractors.

Hans Tronser *(Courtesy J Deere, Mannheim)*

I am indebted to my late friend and Lanz authority, Eric Bolwell, without whose assistance I could not have put together this chapter. Sadly the text was not completed until just after Eric's untimely death. I also wish to acknowledge the contribution made by Bruce Kennedy and Craig Pink.

Tractor engine designs of the 1950s

It is interesting to contemplate that in modern times the entire spectrum of tractors conforms to specific engineering principles. There is therefore little risk of a farmer making a bad choice. But in the 1950s, with tractors ranging from single-cylinder semidiesels to multicylinder petrol–kerosene or diesel designs, selecting the right tractor required considerable research and a fair degree of faith.

The big evolution of tractor designs took place during the first sixty years of the 20th century. By 1960 the classic tractor period had come to an end. All the oddball machines, reflecting the dramatic evolutionary process, had been replaced by conventional diesel-powered units, differing only in peripheral and cosmetic ways to those of today. But as late as the 1950s, the remarkable Bulldogs, Marshalls, Johnny Popper John Deeres, and the multitudes of petrol–kerosene tractors that so reeked of character, were still in production.

In order to gain an understanding of this diversity of design of the 1950s, one example of each tractor/engine type of the period is reviewed in this chapter.

1. 1–CYLINDER PETROL ENGINE

The British Anzani Iron Horse was produced in Hampton Hill, Middlesex, England. This very capable market garden tractor was powered by a single-cylinder air-cooled JAP (JA Prestwick) 412cc engine which under test produced 4.3 belt hp at 2000rpm, but was rated by the manufacturer as 6hp. In place of a conventional clutch, the Iron Horse was provided with a centrifugal clutch which could prove a handful to an inexperienced operator, as it did not engage until about 800 engine rpm. The patented steering was by differential action dog clutches, controlled by levers on the handlebars. This too could prove formidable until the technique was mastered. A comprehensive range of ploughs, cultivators, riggers etc.

was available. The belt pulley was located somewhat awkwardly at the rear of the transmission housing. The drawbar pull of 700lbs at 1.28mph, is not indicative of the overall ability of this well-conceived little market garden tractor.

2. 1-CYLINDER SEMIDIESEL ENGINE

The Lanz Bulldog Model Q is notable as being the final Bulldog medium-weight tractor designed and produced in Mannheim, Germany. It represents the end of a tractor dynasty. The Model Q, with its single-cylinder valveless 2-stroke engine, was rated at 40hp but, as with all semidiesel Bulldogs, its pulling ability was greater than a conventional tractor of similar horsepower. When tested at Marburg the Q exhibited an impressive drawbar pull of 9435lbs at 1.3mph, with a fuel consumption of less than 1 gallon of diesel per hour.

3. 1-CYLINDER FULL COMPRESSION IGNITION DIESEL ENGINE

The Fowler VF English-made crawler featured the same engine as its first cousin, the Field Marshall wheeled tractor. The horizontal, single-cylinder, valveless 2-stroke engine differed from all the other big bore singles by being a full compression ignition diesel. It could be started by hand cranking, using an igniter, or by inserting a shotgun-style cartridge into the breech block then striking the cartridge with a hammer. The resulting energy being directed into the cylinder head literally exploded the engine into life.

A dedicated following of owners in Britain and overseas appreciated the economy and simplicity of the VF crawler. They had nothing but praise for its ruggedness and total reliability, and were obviously prepared to suffer the noise and vibration, which was the penalty of owning a Fowler VF.

Agricultural and earthmoving contractors were attracted to the Fowler VF owing to its suitability for industrial and construction applications. In countries where it was sold, engineering companies designed and fitted an array of bulldozer and ripper attachments custom-built for the VF crawler.

Previous page, top: A British Anzani Iron Horse, owned and restored by Darren Puls.

Previous page, bottom: The single-cylinder JAP air-cooled 4-stroke engine of the British Anzani Iron Horse.

A Lanz Bulldog Model Q. The green and gold colour scheme indicates it was one of the last Model Q Bulldogs to be manufactured after the Mannheim acquisition by Deere and Co. of Moline, USA. Owned by GH Spittle of Australia.

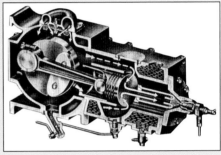

Line drawing of the second-generation Lanz Bulldog engine as in the Model Q. The arrows indicate the action of the loop scavenging system. Unlike the heavy cast piston of the earlier engines, this engine has a flat-headed light alloy piston which negated much of the vibration of its predecessors. *(Courtesy Lanz Archives, Mannheim)*

A Fowler VF owned by Stephen Arbuckle of New Zealand.

4. 2-CYLINDER PETROL–KEROSENE ENGINE

The Chamberlain 40K was an Australian tractor manufactured in Welshpool, Western Australia. The remarkable feature about this big broadacre tractor was its custom-designed 2-cylinder horizontally opposed engine, with its big cylinders protruding on either side of the engine frame. There simply was no other engine in any tractor in the 1950s that resembled the amazingly smooth running 4-stroke Chamberlain power unit. At a mere 1200rpm it delivered 41 belt hp, yet exerted a 5300lbs drawbar pull at 2.86mph, with only 8 per cent wheel

A Chamberlain 40K driven by Mark Puls.

slip. Provided with nine forward and three reverse gears and weighing around 4 tons, this tractor could handle the broadacre implements which were emerging to match the drawbar pull capabilities of the new generation heavyweights. The Chamberlain was a credit to the relatively small Australian tractor industry and presented a serious challenge in its home country to the American and European imports.

In modern times, the Chamberlain 40K and its 2-cylinder successors have become highly collectable, almost to cult status. Although never originally sold outside Australia, many are now found in European and North American collections.

5. 2-CYLINDER DIESEL ENGINE

The Deutz D25 was a product of the giant German conglomerate Klockner-Humboldt-Deutz AG and could trace its tractor ancestry back to 1907. Thus when the D25 was introduced in 1959 it was one of the few tractors in the world that could boast a pedigree of around half a century.

The 1.7L 22hp 2-cylinder diesel was air-cooled, a feature of all Deutz tractor engines from 1952 onwards when the previous water-cooled models were fazed out. Despite the initial hesitation by Deutz agents in hot climate regions such as India, Egypt, Africa and Australia, the air-cooled diesels presented no overheating problems, even in the torrid summer temperatures of these lands.

The D25 featured a delightfully well-spaced gearbox providing eight forward and two reverse gears. The extendable front axle and a multiplicity of rear wheel spacings rendered the tractor suitable for low-height

This D25 was discovered parked in the village of San Valentino in the alpine region of Northern Italy.

row crops. When operating in alpine regions, by extending the wheel width, the tractor's stability could be increased owing to the resultant lowering of its centre of gravity.

Typical of German tractors of the 1950s, a passenger seat was provided on the left side rear mudguard. The example shown is fitted with a hydraulically controlled mid-mounted sickle hay mower.

6. 3-CYLINDER DIESEL ENGINE

The Sheppard Diesel SD3 was manufactured in Pennsylvania by the RH Sheppard Company. The company introduced a range of diesel tractors in 1949 which remained in production until 1956. The tractors, all fitted with Sheppard's own uniquely designed diesel engines, were outstanding considering the company had no earlier associations with the tractor industry.

The SD3, available in row-crop or full-width front axle configurations, was powered by a 3-cylinder, 188cu in, 32hp engine. As with all Sheppard diesel engines, it was based on the indirect injection Lanova (German) design and included Sheppard's own ingenious inline injection pump and non-bypass injector nozzles. The system could be finetuned in the field without recourse to a diesel technician.

The Timken-designed rear-end provided a live pto shaft and live hydraulics. Interestingly, it was identical to that in the Canadian Cockshutt tractors of the same period. A gearbox of four forward and one reverse gears was standard, but an optional eight high speed or slow speed gearbox was available at extra cost.

RH Sheppard produced a custom version of the 3-cylinder diesel engine, designed exclusively as a replacement for the 4-cylinder petrol–kerosene unit as fitted to the International Farmall M.

A Sheppard Diesel SD3, owned by Vern and Grace Anderson of Lincoln City, Nebraska, USA.

Diesel's the Power for Your **M***...

Save 75% on Tractor Fuel Bills
... ease the squeeze on Farm Profits

No Spark Plugs
No Carburetor
No Magneto
with Sheppard
FULL-diesel operation

Pistons are oil cooled. Directionally formed spray distributed in relation to pattern of heat beneath combustion chamber.

Generous cooling areas in head reduce valve temperature.

Full floating wrist pins distribute bearing wear — increase bearing life.

Camshaft is precision ground on all wearing surfaces - heat treated for long life. Removable WET-TYPE cylinder liners for really efficient cooling.

Crankshaft is heat treated steel . . . counter weighted for balance . . . rifle drilled for full pressure lubrication.

Lubricating oil pump insures generous supply of oil to all parts of engine. Oil change required twice a year . . . spring and fall.

Connecting rods matched in sets both for weight and length.

Sheppard Diesel conversion unit ready to drop into place.

Now, this new Sheppard Diesel conversion unit makes is possible for every Farmall "M" owner to profit by the amazing fuel economy of FULL-diesel operation. It has been specially designed for your model "M" tractor, at the same time, retaining all the features that have made Sheppard Diesels famous for dependable, low-cost power throughout the world. Using the simplified Sheppard fuel injection system that can be serviced by any mechanic, this Sheppard Diesel starts and operates efficiently on a wide variety of low-cost fuels . . . usually No. 2 furnace oil or any diesel fuel. The high combustion efficiency of Sheppard's FULL-diesel operation cuts fuel consumption more than half. And, since the fuels used in a Sheppard Diesel cost only about half as much per gallon as gasoline, the net result is a 75% saving on your fuel bill (½ the fuel times ½ the price equals ¼ the cost). Now, this sensational operating economy can be yours without the expense of an entirely new tractor and the trouble of adapting new implements. Convert your Farmall "M" today for greater farm profits tomorrow.

SPECIFICATIONS

Bore		4"
Stroke		5"
Main Bearings		4
Maximum Engine Speeds - full load		1650 r.p.m.
	no load	1735 r.p.m.
Horsepower		Same as a new Farmall "M" with added Diesel lugging power
Governor - Sheppard fly-ball type		5% regulation
Ignition system		full-diesel compression ignition
Fuel		No. 2 furnace oil or any diesel fuel
Starting System		electric starting on fuel oil

A sales pamphlet published by the RH Sheppard Company in the 1950s to promote the sale of the Sheppard 3-cylinder diesel as an alternative power unit for International Harvester's Farmall M.*(Courtesy Lynn Klingaman, Indiana, USA)*

7. 4-CYLINDER PETROL–KEROSENE ENGINE

The International McCormick Deering W4 Standard was one of International Harvester Co's top-selling tractors of the 1950s. At the time, International was the world's largest producer of agricultural tractors; there was a model to suit every type of farming, each considered reliable and well engineered by both farmers and the tractor industry in general. The medium range W4 was available from 1940 until 1953, by which time around 33 000 had been produced. It was exported widely around the world.

The W4 had the same C-152 engine as its stablemate, the Farmall H. The ohv 4-cylinder engine produced 24.87 belt hp at 1650rpm. The drawbar pull was a modest 3297lbs but at the reasonably high speed of 2.21mph.

A slimmed down W4, called the O-4, came equipped with fully enclosed rear mudguards for orchard applications. There were other variants including a yellow industrial version. Its larger brothers, the W6 and W9, were the International tractors most favoured by grain farmers. However the W4 suited the smaller mixed farms where it served as a general purpose tractor.

A fine example of a W4 Standard, owned by Alvin Alderman.

8. 4–CYLINDER DIESEL ENGINE

The Turner Yeoman of England had a V4-configured diesel engine. The cylinders of all other 4-cylinder diesel engines in tractors were arranged in line (with the exception of the Austrian-built 1957 Austro, which had a Warchalowski V4 diesel). Designed by well-known British engineer Freeman Sanders, the compact 40 belt hp engine was originally produced at his Penzance works and installed in Cornish fishing trawlers. It was later manufactured under licence by the Turner Manufacturing Company Ltd of Wolverhampton, England, with certain modifications rendering it appropriate for the Yeoman of England. At 1500rpm the engine developed 40 belt hp and the tractor achieved 5250 drawbar pull at 2.2mph.

During the early 1950s, petrol–kerosene-fuelled engines were still the popular choice for farmers in Britain and North America. Accordingly, during the planning stages in the mid-1940s it was far-sighted of the Turner board to decide upon a diesel engine for their new tractor. By the end of the 1950s the pendulum had swung well and truly to favour diesel power. But by that time the Turner had been relegated to the history books; its pricing structure could not compete with the new Fordson Major diesel tractors and the other diesel units coming into the market at highly competitive prices.

The Turner pictured above has been restored by the author and is part of his collection. Its serial number indicates it was the ninth production Turner assembled.

The right-side bank of cylinders of the Turner engine. The bore and stroke is 3.75 x 4.5in and the vee is set at a 68° angle. Two CAV injector pumps are positioned in the valley of the vee. The tractor was provided with four forward gears and one reverse.

9. 6-CYLINDER PETROL–KEROSENE ENGINE

The Oliver Standard Fleetline 88, with its big, smooth running 6-cylinder engine, was introduced in 1947. The Oliver Corporation of Illinios, USA, made tractor history when it first released its line of excellent 6-cylinder engines back in 1935 in the 70 Series.

The handsomely styled Fleetline Series was the brainchild of Oliver's senior design engineer T Herbert Morrell. The 88's 6-cylinder ohv petrol–kerosene engine produced 44.96 belt hp. The engine block had been built with sufficient internal strength to withstand the extra demands of diesel power and therefore the tractor could be ordered either as a petrol–kerosene or diesel fuelled unit.

An Oliver 88 owned by B and N McKenzie.

In April 1948 an Oliver 88 was tested at Nebraska and produced a drawbar pull of 4.863lbs at 2.51mph. The tractor was noted for the refinement of its engine (rather than power) and the excellence of its six forward, two reverse, two-stage gearbox, with the single change lever engaging either ratio.

The outboard dry disc brakes worked very efficiently, unlike many tractor braking systems of the era. A single wide 'balancing' brake pedal enabled the operator to engage both brakes together, or individually as turning brakes. The attractive side panels were abandoned in the interests of easier maintenance and better cooling in the Super 88, which superseded the 88 in 1954.

10. 6-CYLINDER DIESEL ENGINE

The Massey Harris 744 PD was first manufactured in Manchester, England, in 1948 and later in Kilmarnock, Scotland, at which time the letter 'P' was dropped and it became simply the 744D. The tractor was a British version of the American-built Massey Harris 44. The 744 PD was only available as a diesel unit powered by a British made Perkins P6 diesel—the same engine as used by Fordson in the E27N Major Diesel. The long stroke 6-cylinder Perkins engine of 288cu in displacement produced 42bhp. Even at its maximum governed 1350rpm, it was almost vibration-free. However, the torque characteristic was disappointing, resulting in frequent gear changes when ploughing in undulating country. This situation was exacerbated by the gap between fourth and fifth gears being 5.35mph and 12mph. This left the tractor without a suitable gear for light cultivation or pasture work.

Despite the foregoing, the 744 PD was a pleasant enough tractor to drive. The 'Velvet Ride' seat was well sprung, although suffered from a lack of adequate padding. Visibility from the seat was excellent and the lights provided good vision for night ploughing.

The Massey Harris 744 series did not sell strongly in Britain, with the majority of the 16 606 produced being exported to Australia and African nations. In 1954 the 744D was superseded by the 745D which was powered by the stronger and more modern Perkins 4-cylinder L4 engine.

This Massey Harris 744 PD is part of the comprehensive collection in the Shaw Tractor Shed, Tasmania, Australia.

The row croppers

F arm tractors originally evolved as an alternative to steam traction engines and animals. They were mainly used for hauling cultivating implements and, to a lesser degree, for belt work such as driving threshing mills and corn grinders.

Farmers opposing tractor technology raised the valid argument that, for most weeks in a year, the expensive tractor remained in the shed totally unproductive. When the ploughing and sowing seasons were over there was little a tractor could do until the harvest, apart from occasionally being required to perform belt pulley work. Teams of itinerant labourers (often comprising totally of women) were still required for thinning, weeding, hoeing and, in some instances, harvesting the crops. This represented a considerable cost to farmers on top of the investment in a tractor.

International Harvester Company of Chicago decided to address this problem, and around 1914 commenced experimenting with motor cultivators. Similar experiments were undertaken by other American companies and some European manufacturers. For a while, motor cultivators attracted a following by agriculturists, but within a decade they had almost disappeared, possibly owing to the fact that in most instances they lacked even the limited versatility of regular tractors. They certainly did not contribute to the replacement of manual field workers.

Under the inspired leadership of Bert Benjamin, the design team at International Harvester Company adopted a fresh approach to the problem of the high cost of manual labour. Numerous prototypes were tested in the

desire to produce an all-purpose tractor. In 1923 around twenty examples of the forerunner to the Farmall were tested on farms mainly in the Midwest corn belt. But it was not until a year later that Benjamin was happy with the basic design and the first International Farmall Regular was sold in March 1924.

The concept was an immediate success. The name Farmall was highly appropriate: the new tractor was not only capable of admirably performing all traditional tractor tasks, but it could also enter cornfields, or indeed any row crop cultivation, and, with its front and mid-mounted implements, do the weeding and hoeing along the rows. This effectively dispensed with the need to hire teams of manual labour. The Farmall Regular was powered by International's own ohv 4-cylinder engine of 3.375 x 5in bore and stroke, which developed 18.03 belt hp at 1200 rpm. Progressively, additional Farmall models were introduced. By 1930, 100 000 were in operation around the world and were being produced at the rate of over 200 per day.

Previous page: Allis Chalmers introduced its 6-12 Motor Cultivator in 1918 following a hesitant start to production. This example is fitted with a sulky seat but a range of cultivated implements could be mounted within the four wheels or trailed from the rear. The LeRoi 2-cylinder engine had a 3.125 x 4.5in bore and stroke. Note the ring gear built into the driving wheels. Owned by the Rosenboom family. *(Courtesy R Rosenboom)*

A Farmall F12, owned and restored by the author. Clearly evident are the mounting points along the chassis for attaching mid-mounted implements. Front implements were connected to the steering system, enabling cultivating tynes to be navigated extremely close to delicate young crops. The F12 had automatic turning brakes operated by rods which ran inside the chassis channels connecting the steering to the brakes. In addition, dual short levers manually operated the turning brakes. There was no foot actuated braking system. The single (or dual) front tricycle wheel ran in the centre row and the rear wheels could be readily adjusted to the width of any individual row crop.

In 1932 the Farmall F12 was added to the range. The smallest of the F series, it featured a 16 belt hp engine with a 3 x 4in bore and stroke (which it shared with the International W12). Aimed for the small acreage row cropper, sales rocketed and by 1938, 123 400 F12 units had been sold.

European tractor companies did not pursue the row crop philosophy to any degree. This appears to have been because most row crops in Europe consisted of vegetables grown on small holdings, the owners of which could not have contemplated the purchase of a tractor. Also, by virtue of their high and spindly profile, row crop tractors were only suitable for level country.

An advertisement from a 1954 Hanomag sales brochure. This historically significant German company followed the example set by Lanz in an endeavour to promote row crop tractors in Europe. The Hanomag Row Crop R27 and R35 were every bit as good as their American counterparts and had the advantage of being powered by an economical Hanomag 4-cylinder diesel engine of 26.9 and 34.8 belt hp respectively. However, unlike in North America, when by 1954 row crop tractors accounted for around 50 per cent of total tractor production, tricycle row crop tractors did not sell in great numbers in Europe.

A 1937 CO-OP 2 Row Crop. Confusingly, there were other non-related tractors branded with the CO-OP name. However this particular CO-OP family was designed by Dent Parrett, who also designed the original Parrett and Massey Harris Nos. 1, 2 and 3 tractors. The CO-OP 2 was manufactured by the Duplex Machinery Company of Michigan. Powered by a Chrysler 6-cylinder, 201cu in, side valve engine, the CO-OP 2 Row Crop could be purchased with a cleverly conceived front cultivator into which the tractor was driven. Owned by Jack Cochran.

Henrich Lanz AG was one German company which did test the European market. In 1930 the company produced the Lanz Type HN Dreirad-Hackfrucht-Bulldog. Owing to the position of the side mounted flywheels and the forward facing horizontal cylinder, there was virtually no accommodation for front and mid implements. Only a limited number were sold and the model was discontinued in 1932. In later years, Lanz again endeavoured to create a market for tricycle row crop tractors in Europe, but without success. In the 1950s Hanomag added two tricycle row crop tractors to their range, the models R27 RC and R35 RC. As with the Lanz, only a relatively small number of these tractors were sold.

Anxious to follow the precedent set by International Harvester, all the major North American tractor producers embarked on a program of row crop tractor development. Accordingly, during the 1930s there were scores of row crop tractors available. The trend continued through the 1940s and 1950s.

A 1931 John Deere GPWT. The 339cu in, 2-cylinder horizontal engine had a 6 x 6in bore and stroke and developed 25.36 belt hp. A pto shaft and power lift were advanced features. The GP was the first row crop tractor produced by Deere and Co. Owned by Bart Cushing of New Hampshire. *(Courtesy B Cushing)*

A classic 1948 Massey Harris 30, powered by a Continental 162cu in 34.18 belt hp engine with a 3.4375 x 4.375in bore and stroke. The 30 superseded the 101 Junior in 1947 and was itself superseded by the Model 33 in 1952. Owned by Peter Harris.

Graham Bradley tractors were manufactured between 1937 and 1941 by the Graham Paige Motor Co. of Detroit for the world's largest mail order company, Sears Roebuck. This 1938 row crop version was powered by a 6-cylinder, 32 brake hp, 217cu in Continental engine. Its 4-speed gearbox could propel it along at 22mph or, by overriding the governor, it was capable of 40mph. Owned by Vern and Grace Anderson of Nebraska.

The Oliver Corporation of Charles City, Iowa introduced its Oliver 60 Row Crop in 1940. It was powered by a 4-cylinder, 3.3125 x 3.5in bore and stroke engine which produced 13.85 belt hp. This example is displayed at the Murray Boyes Tractor World Museum at Upper Moutere, New Zealand. The tractor is complete with a mid scarifier and has been totally restored to original condition.

The Ford Motor Co. of England produced the Fordson N All Around row cropper at its Dagenham works with hopes of selling them into the North American market. Very few were sold, mainly on account of the ageing technology of the 4-cylinder, side valve, splash lubricated engine and the 3-speed gearbox, plus the worm gear final drive rear end. Owned by Fred Muscat.

Minneapolis Moline Co. joined the rush to construct a range of row crop tractors and this 1946 RTU lightweight was one of the best. Its 23 belt hp, 4-cylinder engine featured unusual horizontal valves operated by long vertical rocker shafts. Owned by Les Smith of New Zealand.

But not all row crop tractors were of tricycle configuration. In fact it was common practice to offer full width extendible front axles as an alternative to the centre single or dual wheel arrangement. Such tractors provided greater stability than the tricycle, but lacked the same extreme manoeuvrability. Also, it was more time consuming when altering the wheel spacing, as both front and rear wheels had to be adjusted.

A factory drawing of the Lanz 12-20 Row Crop Bulldog. Its single-cylinder engine had a 170 x 210mm bore and stroke with a capacity of 4767cc. As with all single cylinder Bulldogs, the engine was a low compression, valveless semidiesel 2-stroke. There was little room to attach side or front mounted implements. *(Courtesy J Deere archives, Mannheim)*

The versatility of a row crop tractor is evidenced by this 1950 International Farmall M equipped with a two-row corn picker. The rear wheels were readily adjustable to the required row width and the tractor would then progress along the rows depositing the corn into a following trailer. This example, in its working clothes, is owned by R and C Goldsworthy.

There were also 'Hi Crop' tractors, a term coined originally by Deere and Company. With their full width extendible front axles they had all the attributes of the row crop machines but with the added bonus of having an even greater ground clearance. Tobacco and other specialist row crop growers created a demand for these extra high clearance tractors.

The ending of the classic era in 1960 also saw the conclusion of the tricycle row croppers. To this day, however, tractors with high clearance and variable wheel widths are still identified as 'row crop' models.

The John Deere 420 Hi Crop had 32in underbelly clearance and was in production from 1956 to 1958. A mere 610 units were made and those remaining are among the most collectable and rare of all styled John Deeres. The 420 had a vertical 113.3cu in, 2-cylinder engine of 4.25 x 4in bore and stroke, and developed 29 belt hp at 1850rpm. Owned by the author.

The Renault 3042

The giant French vehicle manufacturer Renault first entered the tractor arena in 1919. Its initial offering was the lightweight GP crawler which had been adapted from a World War I military tank design. This was followed in 1920 by a wheeled variant, the HO. Other tractor models followed, including the PE 2 in 1930, and in 1948 the comprehensively equipped Renault 3042 was introduced into the world tractor export market.

The arrival of the 3042 coincided with the proliferation in sales of Renault's British rivals, David Brown, Ferguson and Fordson. The 3042 is often overlooked by contemporary tractor scribes and in historical terms has never received the high profile of the British machines. This is regrettable, as the Renault was an excellent all-purpose medium sized tractor with many fine innovative features.

Standard fittings of the Renault 3042 included comprehensive instrumentation, front and rear lights, full length bonnet side panels and a comfortable sprung seat with back rest. Although the 3042 usually incorporated Renault's own 85 series petrol or petrol–kerosene engine, it could also be powered by either a Perkins L4 diesel or a Hercules DOOD diesel. This choice of engines contributed to the tractor's export potential by broadening its acceptability to various foreign markets.

A range of nine rear wheel pneumatic tyre configurations and three steel wheel types were listed in the catalogue and could be ordered directly from the factory. When coupled with the seven variable wheel track widths, this choice of wheel equipment added significantly to the versatility of the Renault 3042, enabling farmers to option their tractors to suit the particular needs of their farm.

No less than three pto shafts were fitted as standard, at a time when most tractors had only one rear pto. Not only did the 3042 have the conventional rear shaft, it also featured a pto shaft protruding centrally from each side of the tractor. This provided power for driving an implement such as a hay sickle cutter bar, and a belt pulley or other attachment could be operated from the opposite side of the tractor.

The in-built hydraulic system of the 3042 exerted a commendable 2-ton lift on the lower links of the 3-point linkage. Each of the two lift arms were fully adjustable, both vertically and laterally. This provided a wide range of configurations, enabling the optimum setting for a plough or other mounted implement.

A clever spring-loaded tow hook incorporated a variable tensioned instant implement release device. This was designed to protect the tractor and its drawn attachment should an immovable object (such as a stump or rock) be encountered by the implement. Also, using the specially designed drawbar attachment, a trailed implement could be raised out of the ground with the 3-point linkage.

Each export market at that time had its own peculiarities and challenges. In some regions, Renault had difficulty competing against the marketing might of the established corporations such as International Harvester, Fordson and Lanz. Many of these companies had created a strong dealership network and often benefited from a local presence dating back several decades. In some situations the only available outlet for Renault tractors in a foreign rural area was the local Renault car dealer.

The circumstances were entirely different in Renault's home market in France and adjoining countries. Patriotic French farmers appreciated the versatility of the 3042 and frequently preferred to invest in the local product, despite the sales assault from overseas companies, particularly British and German. However, it seemed certain that farmers of any nation who invested in a 3042 were pleased with their purchase and would have had no hesitation in recommending the tractor to their neighbours.

Introduced in 1929, the Renault PE retained the traditional Renault design, with its radiator located at the rear of the engine. It was essential for side panels to be in position in order to direct the flow of air drawn forward from the cockpit and through the radiator, before finally being expelled rearwards. Restored by Dave Bethelson. *(Courtesy A Plunkett)*

The Renault 3042 had clean, neat lines similar to the American-styled tractors of the period. The left-hand side pto shaft is clearly evident; in total, the tractor featured 3 pto outlets. Restored by the late Col Francis.

An advertisement featured in Australian farming journals in 1949 by the local Renault tractor importer.

The 1920 Renault GP, the company's first agricultural tractor, was developed from a light army tank. The 4-cylinder, side valve petrol engine produced a maximum 20hp. This example is owned by the Red Hill Museum, Victoria, Australia.

This specification table was included in the Renault 3042 promotional brochure and listed the three engine options.

SPECIFICATION OF THE RENAULT TRACTOR

	« 85 » ENGINE	PERKINS ENGINE	HERCULES ENGINE
ENGINE	Bore 85 mm.	Bore 88.9 mm.	Bore 107.9 mm.
	Stroke : 105 mm.	Stroke 127 mm.	Stroke 114.3 mm.
	Number of cylinders 4.	Number of cylinders 4.	Number of cylinders 4.
	Cubic capacity 2384 cc.	Cubic capacity 3140 cc.	Cubic capacity 4190 cc.
	Rated speed 1.800 rpm.	Rated speed 1600 rpm.	Rated speed 1800 rpm.
	Centrifugal governor at all speeds.	Vacuum governor limiting speed to 1600 rpm.	Mechanical governor limiting speed to 1800 rpm.
	SOLEX carburettor	CAV injection pump.	Injection pump with plunger piston.
	Oil bath air filter.	Oil bath air filter.	Oil bath air filter.
	Lubrication under pressure.	Lubrication under pressure.	Lubrication under pressure.
	Automatic advance	Automatic advance.	Automatic advance.
	Water cooling circulation pump	Water cooling circulation pump.	Water cooling with circulation pump.
	Electric starter.	Electric starter.	Electric starter.
(coil)	Ignition by distributor.		
Rear power take off standardised (35 mm) in the body of the tractor. (1.378").	Speed - 590 rpm.	Speed - 525 rpm.	Speed - 590 rpm.
Lateral type take oft standardised (35 mm) (1.887") Length (74 mm) (2.913").	Speed of rotation 670 rpm.	Speed of rotation 596 rpm.	Speed of rotation 670 rpm.
Threshing pulley. Diametre 390 mm. (15.354") width 170 mm (6.692").	Belt speed 137 m. per sec. 45 ft. par sec.	Belt speed 12.2 m. per sec. 41 ft per sec.	Belt speed 13.7 m. per sec. 45 ft. per sec.
WEIGHTS Without extra weights and without driver.....	1,800 kilos. 35 cwt 1qr 21 lbs	1,900 kilos. 38 cwt - 20lbs.	2,080 kilos. 40 cwt 3 qrs. 22 lbs.
With maximum weights (front bumper front and rear weights) water filled tyres with-out driver	2,040 kilos. Cwt qrs lbs 51 3 25	2,750 kilos. Cwt qrs lbs 54 0 16	2,895 kilos. Cwt qrs lbs 56 3 27

MULTIPLE PLATE clutch.

FRONT AXLE.
    Oscilating type with adjustable track.

STEERING.
    Worm and wheel type. Outside turning circle maximum track 7.60 (25') minimum track 7.00 m. (23').

BRAKES
    1) on the mechanism - hand brake lever.
    2) on the rear wheel - one pedal for right hand brake and one pedal for left hand brake.

ELECTRICAL EQUIPMENT.
    Diesel Tractors : 6 volt 90 amp/hr. batteries.
    Motor « 85 » Tractors : 6 volt 90 amp/hr batteries.
    Head lights — three (two front and one rear).
    Electric horn. Starter.

HYDRAULIC LIFT.
    Number of cylindres - one.
    Bore 85 mm.
    Number of lifting arms - two.
    Stroke of arms 245 mm. - (9.645").
    Maximum load on arms - 2,000 kilos. - (4.410 lbs).

The Regie Nationale des USINES RENAULT reserve the right to modify without these models.

Evolution of
the David Brown Cropmaster

David Brown, gentleman farmer and industrialist, is remembered as one the great architects of the British tractor industry. His first interest in the production of tractors was kindled in 1933 when he struck up a friendship with Ulsterman Harry Ferguson, who had built the prototype of a revolutionary lightweight tractor.

The outstanding feature of Ferguson's machine was the incorporation of his brilliant patented hydraulic system. David Brown, recognising the marketing potential of the unit, formed a business alliance with Ferguson and arranged to provide the necessary capital to put the tractor into production. The new tractor, to be known as the Ferguson Type A, would be manufactured in an old warehouse in Yorkshire.

In 1936 the Ferguson Type A was launched, at a time when the British farming economy was still reeling from the effects of the Great Depression and banks were hesitant about lending money for tractor purchases. Further, a farmer wishing to acquire a Ferguson Type A, would be obliged to also invest in a range of matched Ferguson 3-point linkage implements, as traditional tractor trailed implements were not compatible with the lightweight tractor.

A total of 1350 Ferguson Type A tractors were built between 1936 and 1939. The first 250 constructed were powered by a Coventry Climax Series E, 4-cylinder side valve engine. Most of the remaining 850 were equipped with a David Brown engine of 2010cc developing 20hp at 1400rpm. The new engine was based on the former Coventry Climax design but the cylinder bore had been increased from 3.125 to 3.25in, with the stroke remaining at 4in. An improved air filtration system was also incorporated.

Owing largely to the depressed British economy, production of the Ferguson Type A was halted in 1939 after a mere 1350 units had been built. By this time the relationship between the two industrialists had soured. Harry Ferguson took his patents across the Atlantic and joined forces with Henry Ford in the US. The Ferguson System was to reappear in late-1939 in the American-built Ford 9N tractor and in 1946 in the British Ferguson TE series.

In the meantime, David Brown had been designing and testing an all-new innovative tractor powered by a 4-cylinder petrol–kerosene ohv engine which, it was claimed, developed 35hp, as opposed to the 20hp engine in the Ferguson Type A. A new four forward speed gearbox and an in-built centre-mounted pto shaft were also features of the new tractor which had not been available with the Ferguson.

The new David Brown, named the VAK 1 (vehicle agricultural kerosene) was released at the 1939 Royal Show in Britain. It received rave reviews from the British farming press and orders poured in. The tractor looked stunning in its bright Hunting Pink colour and farmers warmed to its clean, streamlined appearance.

But the storm clouds had been gathering over Europe and on 3 September 1939 Britain was plunged into World War II. The David Brown tractor factory at Meltham was converted to military production and only a limited number of VAK 1 tractors were assembled.

As part of their contribution to the war effort, David Brown Tractors Limited was encouraged to enter the crawler tractor field, and in 1941 the British Air Ministry

A 1936 photo of a Ferguson Type A, taken during a field demonstration at Herefordshire, England. Note the Ferguson 2-furrow, 12in mouldboard plough attached to the patented 3-point linkage system. It is obvious, from the dangerously exposed lugged wheels, minus mudguard (fender) protection, there was little consideration given to the operator's safety. *(Courtesy S Haughton, R Deering)*

issued the company a contract to produce 185 track-laying airfield tractors. These were to be based upon the agricultural wheeled model VAK 1.

By way of interest, in classic bureaucratic style and following the delivery of the tractors, the Air Ministry decided that it did not in fact require crawler tractors after all. This followed complaints from RAF Wing Commanders about the damage the crawlers were causing to runways. The Ministry paid David Brown to take back and convert the crawlers into wheeled tractors, which were eminently more suited to towing aircraft and other airfield duties. A batch of around 100 crawlers was then custom-built for the Royal Engineers. These were powered by 40hp Dorman diesel engines and designated the DB 4. Reportedly a number were used during the Normandy landings where they hauled armaments and supplies up the beaches that had been unloaded from landing barges.

At the termination of hostilities in 1945, the VAK 1 agricultural wheeled tractor was superseded by the VAK 1A. The updated model was given only minor technical improvements, but with a readily identifiable new front radiator grill.

A significant event of the evolution of the VAK series took place on 21 April 1947 with the release of the VAK 1C Cropmaster. Without doubt, the Cropmaster was the most comprehensively fitted out British tractor of the period. Standard equipment included 3-point linkage, pto shaft, belt pulley, dual upholstered seating, full lighting equipment, electric start, variable wheel track widths, bonnet side panels, six forward speed gearbox, both foot- and hand-operated clutch, underseat tool box, turning brakes and an excellent operator's manual.

During the production life of the Cropmaster (1947–1953) numerous variants were introduced including a tricycle row cropper, a narrow vineyard version, a tug tractor plus the Super Cropmaster and Prairie Cropmaster, the latter being aimed specifically at the North American market.

A noteworthy David Brown milestone was reached with the introduction of the diesel engine VAD Cropmaster in November 1949. When the VAK petrol–kerosene engine was first developed, the design engineers built rigidity and strength into the block in anticipation that it would later be produced as a diesel unit. This was farsighted in the extreme, as in the late 1930s few tractor designers could have envisioned the worldwide swing to diesel tractors that would commence in the early 1950s. The diesel Cropmaster was an instant success with its ease of starting, economy of running and high torque characteristics.

The David Brown on the left is a 1948 VAK 1C Cropmaster (identified by the rounded front casting below the radiator grill) and the tractor on the right is a 1945 VAK 1A (note the narrow mudguards). The two tractors are part of a collection owned by Billy Dass and located on the windswept Isle of Burray in the UK's Orkney Islands. It is unlikely there would be a David Brown collection closer to the North Pole than this!

A David Brown Cropmaster restored by the author and part of his private collection. Its serial number, P444493, indicates that it was manufactured in February 1953 and therefore was one of the last Cropmasters produced. In March of that year the Cropmaster was superseded by the 30C, the first of which still retained the Cropmaster body panels. Note the squared front casting, below the radiator grill, which was a feature of the later Cropmasters, plus the air cleaner inlet pipe located outside the bonnet panel. The tractor has been painted in the correct Hunting Pink colour scheme using basic quick-dry enamel. This example is powered by the David Brown ohv petrol–kerosene engine which develops 35 brake hp.

The David Brown Trackmaster, introduced in January 1950, was virtually a crawler adaptation of the VAK Cropmaster and powered by the same petrol–kerosene engine. The diesel version was introduced in September of the same year. Some of the crawler production experiences, gained with the government contracts during World War II, assisted with the development of the Trackmaster.

Trackmasters were equipped with controlled differential steering and featured a six forward speed gearbox. Both the petrol–kerosene and diesel units could achieve a creditable drawbar pull of 8500lbs at 1.18mph (which roughly equated to the field performance of International Harvester's volume selling T and TD 6 crawlers).

A total of 59 800 of the several Cropmaster variants (excluding crawlers) had been produced by March 1953. The marque was replaced by an excellent new range of 25 and 30 Series tractors, but they lacked the character of the Cropmasters and had only basic tin work, in the interests of economy, which rendered them decidedly less stylish. A 6-cylinder 50hp crawler appeared in mid-1952 and the same engine was used in the 50 D wheeled tractor which made its debut in January 1953.

UNUSUAL FEATURES OF EARLY DAVID BROWNS

From the VAK 1 through to the Cropmaster (apart from the Prairie Cropmaster) the tractors featured an upholstered dual seat arrangement, at a time when most tractors provided only a single steel pan seat. Also, the clutch and brake pedals were located on the right-hand side of the transmission housing. The operator therefore did not straddle the transmission as was customary on other light- to medium-weight tractors.

The turning brakes were activated by individual hand levers, positioned one either side of the dual seat. Plus, an over-centre hand clutch lever (in addition to the foot pedal) was placed behind and to the left of the seat. This enabled the unit to be moved forward without the operator being seated in his tractor, thus avoiding the necessity of having to clamber on and off. This was indeed a welcome feature during stop/start operations if progressing through a field forking, for example, sugar beet or grain sheafs into a trailer. However it was also potentially hazardous, as the operator normally stood on the trailer drawbar, or simply walked alongside the rear wheel, and reached over to work the clutch hand lever to move his tractor.

During World War II, David Brown produced a variation of the VAK designated the VIG. Specifically, the VIG was an aircraft-towing tractor custom-built for the British Royal Air Force. In the postwar period there remained a demand for this type of tractor, not only by airport authorities but also from agricultural contractors. This beautifully restored unit, with its handsome flowing lines, is a 1953 David Brown Taskmaster powered by the 4-cylinder, David Brown ohv petrol–kerosene engine coupled to a fluid drive torque converter. Owned by Merv Hill.

The fluid drive transmission housing fitted to Merv Hill's 1953 David Brown Taskmaster.

The David Brown Trackmaster was given an update in 1953 and renamed the David Brown 30T (pictured). Its Cropmaster lineage was obvious. The crawler, either petrol or diesel powered (30TD), performed admirably in agricultural applications. Some, however, were fitted with heavy bulldozer blades and frequently expected to do the jobs of larger industrial units. As a result both the 30T and 30TD were unfairly criticised by some contractors. The 30 T and 30TD were replaced in 1960 by the 40hp diesel crawler—the 40TD. Owned by L Laing of Tasmania, Australia.

This table will assist enthusiasts in identifying the range of early David Brown tractors.

PREFIXES TO TRACTOR SERIAL NUMBERS

Prefix	Description	Serial
P	— Cropmaster and David Brown 30C	— P10001
P30	— 30C (new series)	— P30/10001
PD	— Cropmaster Diesel and David Brown 30D	— PD10001
PD30	— 30D (new series)	— PD30/10001
SP	— Super Cropmaster	— SP10001
SPP	— Prairie Cropmaster	— SPP10001
PDP	— Prairie Cropmaster Diesel	— PDP10001
TAK }3 / TAG	— Trackmaster and 30T (Kerosene or Gasoline)	— TAK }3/X/10001 / TAG
TAD/3	— Trackmaster Diesel and 30TD	— TAD/3/X/10001
TAD/6	— Trackmaster Diesel 50 and 50TD (6 cylinder)	— TAD/6/X/10001
ITD/3	— 30ITD Industrial	— ITD/3/X/10001
ITD/6	— 50ITD Industrial (6 cylinder)	— ITD/6/X/10001
M	— Cropmaster " M " (less hydraulic lift)	— M10001
MD	— Cropmaster Diesel " M "	— MD10001
R	— Taskmaster and 30IC	— R10001
AM	— 30IC (Air Ministry Specification)	— AM101
RD	— Taskmaster Diesel and 30ID	— RD10001
N	— Cropmaster Vineyard Tractor (Narrow)	— N10001
ND	— Cropmaster Vineyard Diesel Tractor	— ND10001
P25	— David Brown 25	— P25/10001
PD25	— David Brown 25D	— PD25/10001
VAD/6	— David Brown 50D	— VAD/6/10001
HV	— Medium Wheeled Aircraft Towing Tractor	— HV101

The Burly tractors—and me

In the 1950s, Burly was the name of a 26 000 acre sheep and cattle property located in the distant north-west plains of New South Wales, Australia. Under the stewardship of Bill Richardson, Burly was noted for the excellence of its Merino flock and Hereford herd. Some outstanding 21-micron wool and trade steers were produced annually on Burly. I was privileged to spend nearly two years with the Richardson family. My employment was in the capacity of jackeroo, the Australian term for a trainee station manager. During this short but eventful period in my late teens, I was taught many valuable skills and lessons.

I was lucky being a jackeroo on Burly Station back in 1953. At least I think so! I was the sole jackeroo and lived at the homestead with Mr Richardson (or 'Burly Bill', as he was known throughout the northwest) and Mrs Richardson. Had I been jackerooing on the adjoining property, I would have been but one of twenty jackeroos who, although employed under the guise of jackaroos, were in fact a cheap form of labour accommodated in barrack-style huts.

To set the scene: Burly Bill was a giant of a man with hands each the size of a side of beef and a rumbling voice that registered seven on the Richter scale. Mrs Richardson sported a sort of roaring twenties hairstyle (straight out of a Noel Coward play) and smoked Du Maurier cigarettes that protruded from the end of an ostentatious 18-inch cigarette holder. Mine was a lonely life on Burly, despite there being about a dozen or so assorted workers. I was not encouraged to mix with the hired help and a visit to the nearest town, Moree, on my own was strictly off limits.

Being the jackeroo I was given the worst horses to ride. They were hard-mouthed, cantankerous beasts without scruples, their main ambition in life being to toss me into prickly thickets at the slightest provocation. Invariably it was my job to pump the extermination dust down the rabbit holes. I later found out that 'extermination dust' was in fact a friendly name for cyanide. Seems jackeroos were expendable! I was also the unfortunate soul ordered aloft to service the highest of the windmills, particularly if there was a gale blowing. It followed, apparently, that if I could survive the windmill hazards, then I was admirably qualified to be lowered down the 18-metre well to clean out the snakes, frogs, and unidentifiable slimy ooze.

But there was a bright side to my life of servitude—the three Burly tractors. It appeared that in the 1950s, the typical lean, slow talking, laconic stockmen were usually found lacking in their knowledge of any form of transportation that didn't require a bridle, and this included the intricacies of such modern technical marvels as tractors. So it was ordained by Burly Bill that the three tractors were to be my area of responsibility, an acknowledgment of my previous youthful farming experiences in Scotland. The Burly tractors consisted of an ancient Case 15-27 on steel wheels, a brand spanking new Case LA and a little grey Ferguson TEA.

THE FIRST LESSON

It was January, 46°C (115°F) in the water bag, and the Richardsons had departed east in the big Humber Super Snipe for a week of seafood dinners and lazing on the beach. For seven glorious evenings I could loosen my collar and discard the tie as I was served, with only myself for company, at the Burly dinner table. Bliss! But I had a week's rabbit ripping to get through.

The 1923 15-27 Case, mounted on its steel wheels, was retained purely for pulling a ripper used for tearing out rabbit warrens. The warrens were located in long grass which covered dangerously concealed spiky stumps, the remnants of a forest that had been felled a century previously. To take a pneumatic tyred tractor in among the

Case 15-27

Period of manufacture: 1919–24
Total production: 17 628
Engine: ohv, cross mounted
Fuel: petrol–kerosene
Cooling: liquid
Hp: 27 rated belt
Rpm: 900
No. of cylinders: 4
bore and stroke: 4.5 x 6in
Gears forward: 2
Gears reverse: 1
Drawbar pull: 3440lbs at 2.05mph
Weight: 6350lbs

A line drawing of a Case 15-27 taken from early 1920s Case promotional material.

stumps would have been asking for trouble. It was therefore Burly Bill's dogma that only the steel wheeled Case 15-27 would be used for ripping.

Anyone who has ever driven a 1923 15-27 Case, with its transverse mounted engine, would be aware that the exhaust manifold runs east-west and is located just inches from the operator's knees. I can tell you—these old Case tractors ran *hot!* Even in the cool of the evening the exhaust manifold would glow a ghostly red.

As a consequence, driving the Case during the heat of midsummer could be likened to sitting alongside a searing blacksmith's forge—I even got blisters on my knees and forehead. Then there was the constant bedlam of sound that roared from the stubby exhaust pipe, the bone-jarring jolting caused by the steel wheels, and the dust—not to mention the hand cranking and wearisome heavy steering, resulting in aching wrists and shoulders.

Can anyone blame me, after my second day alone, for leaving this mobile torture machine in its shed and deciding to continue the ripping with the big, new, shining Case LA? After all, Burly Bill was off enjoying himself so why should I slave away on the old 15-27? Such was my somewhat illogical and immature reasoning. At the touch of a button, the gleaming Flambeau Red Case LA burbled into life. I reversed it gently out of the shed, using the silky smooth, hand-operated over-centre clutch and hooked it up to the ripper.

Dan, the station mechanic, came running across from his workshop waving his arms, aghast that I was intending ripping with the LA. 'Don't worry,' I brazenly assured him, and headed for the rabbit warrens out in Chinaman's Paddock, some 13km distant.

A mob of thirty or so of the resting horses had gathered near the gate between Chinaman's and Mitchell Plains. The wretched things were eyeing me and would gallop through in a flash if I just drove up and opened the gate. Thankfully, the Case LA had an in-built secret weapon for dealing with just such contingencies. I raced around the horses with the big kerosene engine howling and abruptly cut off the ignition with the spark control. Then I quickly pushed the lever back again and *bang*, unburned gas in the exhaust system exploded with the shattering noise of a cannon. The horses took off back down the

Case LA

Period of manufacture: 1940–52
Total production: 41 063 (includes all variants)
Engine: ohv
Fuel: petrol–kerosene
Cooling: liquid
Hp: 52.5 rated belt
Rpm: 1100
No. of cylinders: 4
Bore and stroke: 4.625 x 6in
Gears forward: 4
Gears reverse: 1
Drawbar pull: 6659lbs at 2.26mph
Weight: 7621lbs

A Case LA identical to the Burly Case. Owned by the Kurtz family.

paddock, neighing and bucking, leaving me to take the tractor through the gate without a hassle.

I commenced ripping a 2-hectare rabbit warren amid the shoulder high coolah grass in Chinaman's Paddock, with what I considered to be care and diligence. The big machine rocked and swayed as it relentlessly criss-crossed the area with the 3-tyne ripper, effectively destroying the warren. That is, until a huge jet of water went shooting high into the air.

The rear tyres of the Case LA each contained around 40 gallons of water ballast. With a hole in the right side tyre big enough for a water-melon to pass through, the 40 gallons came out in the manner of a burst municipal water main. An evil, razor sharp spiky stump, now wet with water, grinned triumphantly up at me.

What a situation—a perfectly good, new tyre ruined, a shiny new Case LA with a lean like a crooked gate, a 13-kilometre walk back to the home-stead under the blazing sun and my job almost certainly on the line. Great!

Dan guessed what had occurred as soon as he observed a thoroughly dejected and perspiring jackeroo gratefully limping into the shade of his workshop. His 'I told you so' expression and the shaking of his head did nothing to ease my sore feet and utterly demoralised ego.

Early the next morning, Dan left in the Austin 3 tonner for Moree to pick up an expensive new tyre and tube. Upon his return, we spent the entire remainder of the day under the torrid sun out at Chinaman's Paddock wrestling with jacks and the massively heavy wheel. The new tyre fought us every inch of the way. Dan was not amused, his sullen mood only bright-ened by the prospect of my early sacking upon Burly Bill's return.

The following day, chastened and wiser, I recommenced ripping—this time with the ancient 15-27 and its puncture-proof steel wheels!

A week later, following dinner, I sat with the Richardsons sipping coffee in the drawing room, uncomfortable in my once-again adorned tie—mandatory despite the sultry heat of the evening. After enquiring politely about their week at the coast, I summoned up the necessary courage to mention the tragedy of the Case tractor tyre.

Burly Bill, with a couple of pre-dinner rum-and-waters under his belt, was about to explode. The cat disappeared from its chair and Mrs Richardson turned unusually pale. I quickly forestalled the coming storm by piously stating that the reason for violating the rules and taking out the new LA had been my concern for the welfare of the old 15-27. I explained I had detected an alarming knocking noise that had developed in the innards of its engine (safe ground here because a 15-27 *always* had strange knocks) and had used my initiative, precisely as I was frequently being encouraged to do.

Further, and with no small degree of martyrdom, I went on to describe how, following the unfortunate accident with the LA, I had adjusted the magneto timing of the 15-27 and surprisingly the knocking noise had disappeared. So I had grimly battled on with the old tractor, despite its perverse idiosyncrasies being the reason for my sprained shoulder and wrist. After all, the job *had* to be done.

Mrs Richardson (bless her) immediately voiced her admiration for my dedication to duty and expressed her concern for my allegedly damaged shoulder and wrist. Her lance-like cigarette holder was used to emphasise the point, daring the huge bulk of Burly Bill to disagree with her. He subsided back into his chair and irritably tinkled the bell for another rum. His expression suggested that while he had lost that round, I would keep. Inwardly, I realised that the entire episode had taught me an

Ferguson TEA 20

Period of manufacture: 1947–56
Total production: 517 651 (includes all variants)
Engine: ohv
Fuel: petrol
Cooling: liquid
Hp: 18.6 rated belt
Rpm: 2000
No. of cylinders: 4
Bore and stroke: 3.15 x 3.62in
Gears forward: 4
Gears reverse: 1
Drawbar pull: 2400lbs at 2.75mph
Weight: 2500lbs

A Ferguson TEA 20, identical to the unit on Burly. Owned by Alan Latimore.

important lesson—don't bend the rules whilst working for Burly Bill. My employment at Burly Station was secure—for the moment.

THE SECOND LESSON

There was a young Dutch carpenter working on Burly in 1953 whose name was Johnny Hindman. He told me how he had changed his name by deed poll from 'Arseman'. Understandable, I thought. Johnny had a BSA single-cylinder 500cc motorcycle which he wished to sell.

By now a feeling of rebellion was brewing in my innards. Burly Bill's philosophies of not encouraging jackeroos to go to town on their own and not to fraternise with the hired help were forming seeds of discontent. After all, I was now 18 years of age and listened with awe to the tales told around the campfire each morning of some of the delights to be experienced in the nearby town of Moree!

I handed Johnny Hindman a bundle of my hard-earned cash in exchange for his BSA motorcycle. Now I would be able to experience a new-found freedom. My horizons had suddenly extended beyond the Burly boundary fence.

But there was a penalty to pay. Burly Bill and Mrs Richardson were not amused by the expression of defiance manifested by my purchase of the motorcycle. Indeed, not a comment was directed to me at the dinner table one fateful Friday evening as I mentioned my intention of visiting Moree the following afternoon.

I toiled the mandatory hours on Saturday morning, then showered and changed into town clothes. Ready to depart for town and preparing to swing my leg over the BSA, I became enveloped in a large shadow. It was Burly Bill. He stabbed a finger in my direction and rumbled a warning about me being back in time to fuel the Fergy at the windmill at midnight.

Moree in the early 1950s was a fairly wild outpost of civilisation, beyond which there were just vast empty plains with homesteads scattered here and there. The tall cowboys, under their broad hats, routinely rode into town on Friday nights to commence their weekend of debauchery. This meant the pubs enjoyed a roaring trade and it triggered the police paddy wagon to go out on patrol.

There may have been fleshpots in Moree but I certainly failed to discover them. A lemon squash at the saloon bar of the Max Hotel followed by a banana split at the Monterey Cafe could hardly be construed as high living. However, I do confess to being thoroughly smitten and indeed I experienced an unfamiliar feeling of pure infatuation whilst at the open air cinema. There I discovered the allure of the lovely young Leslie Caron as she danced her way through the Hollywood musical

An American in Paris. In fact I simply could not get her out of my mind—and that proved to be the problem which was later to unfold.

On the return motorcycle ride to Burly, under the stars and along the rough dusty trails, I sang the songs from the movie over and over. But, being mindful of Burly Bill's stern warning, I made a point of arriving back at the station at midnight. I could sympathise with Cinderella. Having parked the BSA in the shed, I climbed aboard the Jeep, in which I had previously placed two 4-gallon drums of petrol for fuelling the Ferguson tractor, and drove off in its direction.

The little grey TEA 20 Ferguson tractor, normally used for hauling a trailer around the place or mustering the horses each morning in the night paddock (if you follow me), was on this occasion mounted upon a 4-wheel trailer in the Out Station paddock. The windmill mechanism had failed, therefore the Ferguson drove a specially rigged pump-jack by means of a belt pulley, from its elevated position upon the trailer. As there were cattle in the paddock, it was essential that water from the bore be kept flowing 24 hours a day, which meant the Ferguson had to be fuelled three times every 24 hours. I knew that Dan, the station mechanic, would have fuelled it at 4pm and it was my job to fuel it at midnight.

I arrived at the windmill 30 minutes behind time, but the Fergy was still doing its stuff up on the trailer. I have to be perfectly honest at this point and state quite simply that my mind was not on the job. I was still enamoured by the glamorous Miss Caron and it was she upon whom I was concentrating—not the Ferguson!

The golden rule when fuelling a petrol tractor, especially when the fuel tank is positioned above the exhaust manifold, is to stop the engine. Well, I was by this time in need of sleep and, as previously stated, my mind definitely elsewhere. So I did not stop the engine. With an opened can of petrol on the trailer waiting its turn, I splashed the contents of the second container into the fuel tank. It had to happen. There was a blinding flash, a red hot whoosh and a fireball blasted me off the trailer and onto the ground—on fire! Fortunately I landed right alongside one of the water troughs, into which I nimbly plunged. It did the trick in dousing the flames, but then I had to immediately scramble out and back away, as the whole area was, by now, burning fiercely. In the epicentre of the conflagration was the Fergy, still aloft upon the trailer.

Twenty minutes later, following a wild drive in the Jeep, I pounded, shouting, on the door of Dan's cottage. A shocked Dan emerged.

'Quick, the Fergy's on fire,' I yelled hysterically.

Clad only in blue striped pyjamas and long wellington boots, Dan jumped into the passenger seat of the Jeep, clasping a fire extinguisher to

A photo, taken in 1953, of the Burly Jeep with the author, aged 18 years, at the wheel. *(Courtesy A King)*

his bosom. I slammed the accelerator hard. As we hurtled back towards the disaster area, narrowly avoiding sleeping cows, the night sky ahead was lit up like a fairground.

When we arrived at the scene, Dan's assessment of the situation was that it would be a waste of good fire extinguisher spray to use it on the now smouldering remains. What had not burned had melted. Of the trailer, there remained only the charred remnants and the tractor was little better. Dan turned his back to the glow and warmed his backside. 'Don't fancy your job having to tell Burly Bill,' he smirked.

At the Sunday morning breakfast table I enquired of Mr and Mrs Richardson if they had heard the excitement during the night. They had not! So I took a deep breath and unburdened my sins. This was the opportunity Burly Bill had been waiting for ever since he had been out-manoeuvred over the burst Case tyre affair. Again Mrs Richardson came to my rescue. She scrutinised my lack of eyebrows and my singed hair.

'You poor dear. It must have been an appalling shock for you.' She placed a protective arm around my shoulder and glared at her husband.

A month later, I apologetically told the Richardsons I would be leaving Burly as I wished to head north on my motorcycle, where, it was rumoured, land was almost being given away. The Northern Territory, my intended destination, lay over 3000 kilometres to the North. Burly Bill had no objections—whatsoever!

Spare parts

This final chapter brings together a condensed assortment of random classic tractor information, ranging from trivia to important facts.

THE ATHENS PLOW COMPANY

By 1928 the Fordson Model F had risen to become the world's undisputed top-selling tractor, with around 750 000 produced. This figure has never been exceeded by a single model of any tractor.

The Model F was basic in the extreme and, like the Ford Model T car, had virtually no factory options available. As a result, a whole new industry developed, mainly in the USA but also overseas, producing attachments and refinements for the tractor. These ranged from crawler tracks to improved carburettor and ignition systems, industrial attachments and of course agricultural implements.

The Athens Plow Company of Ohio produced a twin disc plough specifically for mounting to the Fordson Model F. The kit included an extension for the front axle. This placed the furrow wheel further to the right, thus providing space for the offset discs which were located midway between the axles.

The idea was excellent, as the two rear wheels remained up on the 'hard', keeping the tractor level. This was an important consideration for tractors with engines, such as the Fordson 4-cylinder side valve unit, dependant on splash feed lubrication. The lever system for raising and lowering the discs also worked well and was placed conveniently to the operator's right side.

PISTON SPEED

The speed of a piston in an engine is calculated by multiplying the length of stroke x engine rpm x 2 (i.e. two movements per crankshaft revolution). So to determine, for example, the piston speed of an International 4300 tractor fitted with a 6-cylinder turbo-charged diesel engine, having a 5.375 x 6in bore and stroke and a maximum governed 2000 rpm, proceed as follows:

6in stroke x 2000 rpm = 12 000

thus 12 000 x 2 = 24 000in per minute

therefore 24 000 ÷ 12 = 2000ft per minute

The piston speed of the International 4300 diesel engine is therefore 2000ft per minute.

THE UNITED

The United tractor has an interesting history. It was designed and produced by Allis Chalmers specifically as a budget tractor for the United Tractor and Equipment Corporation of Chicago. The Corporation consisted of a number of farm machinery retail organisations that had grouped together for the purpose of being able to market a tractor that could compete in price with the sales-dominating Fordson. By forming a cartel, it was hoped they could take advantage of the economy of scale principle, thus being able to offer a tractor at a competitive price.

The United was produced for just over 12 months, when it was given a name change and became the Allis Chalmers Model U. For transport purposes, David Hawkins has removed the wheel grip lugs of his well presented example of a rarely seen 1930 United.

To the surprise of the industry, the Ford Motor Company discontinued the manufacturing of Fordsons in the USA in 1928. Plans had been made for the relocation of the entire Fordson tractor plant to Cork, Ireland. Therefore, when United came onto the scene in 1929, its main opposition was not Fordson, but International. The matter only became the subject of conjecture when the United Tractor and Equipment Corporation collapsed just a year later in 1930.

Allis Chalmers, in the worrying position of being left with hundreds of partly assembled United tractors and their already-purchased Continental engines, decided to market the unit as an Allis Chalmers Model U. The United badge, cast into the radiator top, was changed to Allis Chalmers and the Allis Chalmers name removed from the radiator sides.

The United (or AC Model U) was powered by a Continental S10 engine of 283.7cu in capacity, which developed 35.04 pto hp and achieved 3679lbs drawbar pull at 2.61mph. It was provided with four forward gears and one reverse. In 1932 the Model U was repowered with an Allis Chalmers designed engine, built by Waukesha, of 300cu in capacity, which was upgraded to 318cu in from serial No. 12001. Production continued until 1952.

HOW TO MAKE STARTER IGNITERS

First, you'll need a sheet of thick blotting paper. Cut the sheet into pieces, each approximately 55 x 40mm (2 x 1½in). Dissolve 85g (3oz) of potassium nitrate into 500ml (16fl oz) of warm water. Soak the pieces of blotting paper in this solution. Remove and leave to dry on a towel in sun.

FRICTION DRIVE

The first-ever International tractor to proceed beyond experimental stage was the International Friction Drive in 1907. The drive from the engine to the transmission was by the friction engagement of non-geared flat surface drivers. The entire engine was moved fore and aft on a slide by the operator, through a system of levers. The successor to the Friction Drive featured geared drive forward motion, but retained friction engagement for reverse. Eventually all the early International tractors became fully gear driven.

Friction drives of differing designs were used in a number of early tractors, including the Heider, Armington, Eason-Wysong, Elgin, Ebert-Duryea, and GO, but were gradually fazed out in favour of direct gear drives. However, the friction drive reappeared in the 1940s, but in a different guise. The Australian engineering company of Malcolm Moore Industries Ltd produced a range of earthmoving machines using farm tractors as a base. One such unit was the cable-operated Moore front-end loader fitted to a Fordson tractor, which included a friction drive mechanism.

The Moore cable loader, actually conceived in the 1930s, was a bizarre yet ingenious contraption produced at a time when hydraulics were

A 1908 15hp International Friction Drive, which used friction engagement for both forward and reverse travel. Owned by Les Noll.

The Malcolm Moore loader has the appearance of an engineering nightmare, however in the 1930s, when it was conceived, it actually represented cutting edge technology. The parallelogram bucket linkage was certainly ahead of its time. Owned by Athol Ruhl.

replacing cable drives. (In defence of Malcolm Moore, it should be stated that the company was amongst the world's first to fit a front-end loader—as distinct from a front dozer—to a wheeled tractor, and went on to produce a range of first-class hydraulic loaders in the 1950s.)

The lift arms of the Moore loader were raised by a cable winch, driven indirectly by friction engagement. The belt pulley on the right of the Fordson tractor was replaced by a smaller diameter flat surface driver which engaged, by friction, a pulley wheel on a shaft, which in turn transmitted the drive by a chain to the cable winch for raising the loader arms. The speed of the descent of the bucket was controlled by a wooden block

A 1948 Fordson Major E27N Roadless half track in the author's private collection. Tractor enthusiasts not experienced with these tractors usually imagine that the steering would be even heavier than the conventional wheeled Major. To the contrary—the steering is surprisingly precise and responsive and, for some illogical reason, seemingly lighter with the half track configuration. The characteristic Fordson 'kick back' remains, however, and operators soon learn to wrap their thumbs around the outside of the steering wheel to avoid the inevitable sprained (or broken) thumb.

acting as a brake on the driven flat pulley. The bucket tip mechanism was in the form of a crude mechanical locking pin, which was released by the operator pulling on a cable-connected lever.

With cables whizzing around and the almost-zero forward vision, on account of the winch mechanism structure, an operator suffered both physical and mental exhaustion by the end of a shift. Added to the driver's woes was the absence of power steering—and a Fordson was heavy to steer even without a loader and a full bucket!

ROADLESS HALF TRACKS

Roadless Traction Ltd of Middlesex, England, produced half tracks and full tracks for a variety of manufacturers. In the 1930s, Bristol, Ransomes and Rushton tractors all used Roadless track equipment. Roadless half tracks could be ordered to fit virtually any 2-wheel drive tractor but they were mainly fitted to the British-made Fordson Majors.

Initially a batch of Fordsons so equipped was produced for Welsh upland farmers whose arable fields were steep and of a sticky clay consistency. During damp weather (most of the time) conventional wheeled tractors had difficulty in obtaining traction. Few of the farmers could afford expensive conventional crawlers such as Caterpillar or Fowler. The Roadless half track Fordsons were found to be ideal for negotiating the slippery hill country and could be purchased at an affordable price.

Although constituting a tiny percentage of the overall Fordson Major sales, the half tracks established a niche market and a number were even sold for export.

The author's 1957 Chamberlain Champion 6G, rebuilt from a rusted-out hulk into a Tail End Charlie replica. Not surprisingly, this unit is his favourite choice when tractor trekking. The Perkins L4 diesel engine is matched to the dual ratio transmission, providing six forward gears. The high top gear enables a safe highway speed to be maintained without frustration to other vehicle drivers. The original Charlie is preserved for posterity in Whiteman Park Museum, Perth, Australia.

Tail End Charlie

A practically stock-standard Chamberlain Champion farm tractor travelled 17 930km in 19 days, over some of the roughest trails in the world, serving as a recovery vehicle during the 1957 Around Australia Mobilgas Trial. It rendered assistance to scores of rally competitors and towed damaged cars a total of more than 1600km.

Despite frequent stops to haul vehicles out of bogs and to upturn dozens of capsized cars, Tail End Charlie, as the Champion was known, covered the long haul of 1660km from Darwin to Mount Isa in 22 hours. This represented an average speed of almost 46mph.

Prior to the 1957 event, Charlie had completed 38 600km in previous rallies and 3000 hours of farm work!

SANDSTONE ESTATES AND A WORLD RECORD

Sandstone Estates, located in South Africa, is a world-class example of modern agricultural business at its very best. Within the span of a decade, and under the guidance of Wilfred Mole, 6382 hectares of scant, unproductive grazing country has been turned into a huge, bountiful garden. Each year 10 000 tons of natural animal manure are ploughed into the soil, resulting in the production of outstanding yields of high quality grain and other crops. In addition, the property runs 1000 head of shining beef cattle. The farm supports 200 employees and has a fleet of forty-two modern tractors.

Whilst the above statistics are undoubtedly impressive, tractor enthusiasts are likely to be even more impressed when they learn that Sandstone owns a superb collection of 140 vintage tractors and twenty steam locomotives, of which nine have been completely restored. A Guinness world record was established at Sandstone Estates on 10 April 1999 for the greatest number of tractors (106) ploughing at the one time in the same field. The Sandstone record was beaten at Yass, Australia, on

15 April 2001 when 298 tractors were officially recognised by the Guinness adjudicators.

Then on 20 April 2002 a successful attempt was made, again at Sandstone Estates, to beat the Australian record and return it to South Africa. The new world record stood at a seemingly unbeatable 755 tractors. The South African record was again shattered, however, this time by the Republic of Ireland; on 4 August 2002 a staggering 1832 tractors were officially recorded all ploughing in the one field simultaneously.

Sandstone Estates promotional material.
(Courtesy Penelope R Coleman)

As the future unfolds, perhaps new records will be achieved. Whether this occurs or not, the entire vintage tractor fraternity from all nations owes a debt of gratitude to Sandstone Estates for initiating the Guinness challenge. The intense interest which it created in the international media served to focus the attention of the world on the importance of preserving old tractors and regarding them as national heritage items.

STATISTICS FOR 1957
World tractor populations
USA: 4 500 000
Britain: 400 000
Africa: 152 000

World tractor exports
Percentages represent that country's international export market share.
USA: 23 per cent
Britain: 50 per cent
Germany: 16 per cent

THE FORGOTTEN SQUIRE TRACTORS

The name of Raimond Ash Squire is unlikely to be familiar to tractor enthusiasts or even to tractor historians. This is regrettable, for it is the name of an Australian farmer and engineer who designed two different models of exceptional tractors during the 1920s and 30s. Had misfortune beyond his control not intervened, the name Squire might have been added to the list of great tractor innovators.

The first of the two models was the Squire Quad Drive powered by a 40hp 4-cylinder Purcell petrol engine. It was built by Purcell Engineering Company Ltd (the company that had earlier taken over the Caldwell Vale tractor plant in New South Wales, Australia). The Quad Drive had similarities to the Caldwell Vale (see page 43) and shared the characteristics of 4-wheel drive and 4-wheel steer, but was a totally different tractor.

Following impressive prototype tests conducted at Hawkesbury Agricultural College in 1917, the Australian Imperial Military Forces placed an order for six of the machines, which were to serve as artillery tractors in France. Squire was obliged to borrow heavily to raise the necessary security before Purcell would proceed with the building of the tractors. In early 1918, as the Quad Drives neared completion, Squire received a curt telegram from the government stating that the order for the tractors had been cancelled owing to the likelihood of a forthcoming armistice.

This came as a devastating blow to Squire. No compensation was offered and he did not have the necessary funds to instigate a court challenge. The bank with which he had negotiated the loan moved in and took possession of all the Squire assets.

In 1930, following some years of resurrecting his financial circumstances, Squire caused a sensation at the Sydney Royal Show when he displayed his latest creation, the ingenious Squire Auto Plough. This was a 3-wheeled

This 1916 photo shows Raimond Ash Squire with his young son Fred, standing alongside the prototype Quad Drive which is loaded with the wool clip of Red Braes Station, Quirindi, Australia. The third person is Jack Harbin, who was killed shortly after in the trenches at Yepres, France, during the closing days of World War I. *(Courtesy Ron Squire)*

tractor powered by a 40hp, Continental Red Seal, 4-cylinder petrol engine mounted over the front two driving wheels. The feature which made the Auto Plough distinctly different was the set of nine 30in-diameter plough discs, located under the belly of the tractor, that power rotated at a speed 16 per cent faster than the drive wheels. The rear steer wheel was offset and followed the left side front wheel in the last furrow. A pto shaft, extending from the right side of the engine, supplied the drive by a series of shafts and two gearboxes to the disc axle. This in turn was provided with downward pressure by a pair of springs, which also served as a stump jump action.

The Auto Plough worked brilliantly. Tests carried out in the tropical regions of Australia on sugar cane plantations gave unprecedented results. The tractor was able to bury cane trash in one pass and undertake deep drainage cultivation more ably than by any previous method. However in 1930 the rural sector was suffering grievously from the effects of the economic depression. Farmers simply could not raise a loan from the bank to purchase such sophisticated equipment. Once again, Squire was in

The Squire Auto Plough, with its power rotating discs built into the tractor chassis, was not totally unique. The 1916 Cleveland Motor Plow also featured powered discs. This photo has been kindly made available by Ron Squire, the third and youngest son of Raimond Ash Squire, who worked closely with his father and brothers on the Auto Plough project.

financial difficulty. Mort's Dock Ltd, the heavy engineering company which had been making the Auto Plough for Squire, not surprisingly demanded payment for its efforts. Once again, Raimond Squire was obliged to abandon a promising engineering project, which had the potential to contribute significantly to mechanised farming.

Thus the saga of the Squire tractors ends on a reflective note. What if the government had not cancelled the contract for the six Quad Drives? What if Squire had received a major injection of funds from a wealthy backer for the Auto Plough? We shall never know.

THE PLYMOUTH/SILVER KING

Plymouth, Ohio, was just another small US Midwestern town in the early 1930s, except that it was almost totally dependant on the fortunes of the local engineering works, Fate Root Heath Company, for its existence. The company manufactured petrol-engined shunting locomotives and was the town's major employer. As a consequence of the Great Depression, the market for shunters evaporated, leaving the Fate Root Heath board with the prospect of closing down the factory (and thus the town) or diversifying into new activities.

Being situated in the centre of a vast farming area, the company decided to enter the tractor business. Luke B Biggs, an ex-farmer with a thorough understanding of tractors, was recruited to head-up the design team. Within an amazingly short space of time, the first production Plymouth tractor was ready for delivery in 1932.

The Plymouth was a lightweight machine designed for use on smaller acreages, or as a utility tractor for larger farms. The engine chosen was the acclaimed Hercules 1XB 4-cylinder side valve, matched to a four forward speed gearbox. The 25mph top speed rendered the tractor highly suitable for hauling wagonloads of produce to neighbouring centres. Row croppers of both 3- and 4-wheel configuration were introduced, plus a variation of wheel types and sizes.

In 1934, the Chrysler Corporation alleged that Fate Root Heath's use of the name Plymouth constituted a breach of copyright, and brought a law suit against the company. The giant vehicle company produced the Plymouth car and claimed ownership of the name. In court, Fate Root

A 1936 Silver King R44 participating in the successful Guinness world record attempt for the greatest number of tractors ploughing simultaneously in the one field, held at Yass, Australia, in 2001. The 'R44' indicates the tractor was originally sold with rubber (pneumatic) tyres, the rears having a diameter of 44in. Owned by Trevor Pain.

Heath was able to prove it had manufactured a range of Plymouth trucks during the 1920s and the judge therefore dismissed the case.

However, it was decided to change the name of the tractor anyway, to Silver King, on account of its colour. It seems the company had an over-abundance of silver paint, a legacy from its pre-tractor days. A broad range of technically interesting Silver King tractors were produced up until 1954, by which time close to 9000 of the marque were performing sterling service, mainly on Midwest farms, with some being used in industrial applications.

ALANSON HARRIS

The board of Massey Harris Ferguson Ltd (created in 1954 as the result of a merger between Harry Ferguson Ltd, UK and Massey Harris Ltd, Canada) determined in December 1957 to drop the name of Harris and become simply Massey Ferguson Ltd. Accordingly, the name of Alanson Harris, who joined forces with Hart Massey in 1891 to form the now historic firm of Massey Harris Company Ltd, was relegated to the history books.

THE HART PARR 18–36

The Hart Parr Company of Charles City, Iowa, was one of the very early pioneers in the farm tractor industry. Its first experimental model, built in 1901, was typically massive in construction and powered by a 30hp 2-cylinder petrol engine with a bore and stroke of a whopping 9 x 13in. The flywheel weighed 1000lbs! A range of production models followed, each with 2-cylinder engines of varying capacity, until in 1927 the Model 28-50 was introduced. This had twin 2-cylinder engines arranged side by side.

As part of a marketing strategy, the Hart Parr 16-30 and 18-36 tractors were given the names New Zealand Special and Australian Special, respectively, when exported to those countries. The aim was to infer that these tractors had been specially modified to suit local conditions. In actual fact their specifications were more or less identical to those of the company's regular tractors.

Although completely outdated by the 1920s, the old styled Hart Parr tractors proved so reliable and mechanically sound that production continued through to 1930. In 1929 Hart Parr merged with the Oliver Chilled Plow Company, Nichols and Shepard Company and American Seeding Machinery Company to form the Oliver Farm Equipment Corporation. A new range of multicylinder tractors was created, some of which were branded Oliver-Hart-Parr. In Canada they were rebadged as Cockshutts.

It is generally believed that HW Williams, the Hart Parr sales manager, was the originator of the term 'tractor'. This is incorrect. George H Edwards of Chicago patented the name in 1890—patent No. 425 600.

A Hart Parr 18-36, fitted with a chaff screen, magnificently restored by Norm McKenzie.

HOWARD TRENCH DIGGER

The great farm machinery pioneer Arthur Clifford Howard is remembered for his innovative development of the rotary cultivator and his unique Howard DH 22 tractor (see page 59). He is less well-known for his activities in England, including the creation of the Platypus 30 Crawler tractor in the mid-1950s. But undoubtedly his most fascinating conception was the Howard Trench Digger and Pipe Layer.

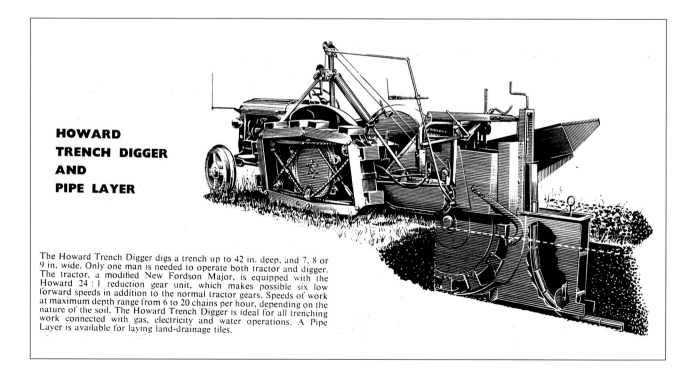

HOWARD TRENCH DIGGER AND PIPE LAYER

The Howard Trench Digger digs a trench up to 42 in. deep, and 7, 8 or 9 in. wide. Only one man is needed to operate both tractor and digger. The tractor, a modified New Fordson Major, is equipped with the Howard 24 : 1 reduction gear unit, which makes possible six low forward speeds in addition to the normal tractor gears. Speeds of work at maximum depth range from 6 to 20 chains per hour, depending on the nature of the soil. The Howard Trench Digger is ideal for all trenching work connected with gas, electricity and water operations. A Pipe Layer is available for laying land-drainage tiles.

MCCLAREN–BENZ OIL TRACTOR

History was made in 1923 when the German automotive company Benz Sendling announced the first ever agricultural tractor powered by a full compression ignition diesel engine. Initially the tractor was built as an unwieldy 3-wheeled unit, with the rear centrally-mounted wheel driven by a chain from the gearbox. The 30hp engine featured two cylinders mounted vertically, with provision for igniters for each cylinder as an aid to starting. From 1925 the tractor was configured as a conventional 4-wheeled unit with rear wheel drive.

J and H McClaren Ltd of Leeds, England, entered into a licensing arrangement in 1927 with Benz Sendling. This resulted in the diesel tractors being partly manufactured at the Midland Engine Works in Leeds. No records have yet been unearthed indicating the percentage of the English components, but it is believed to have included the engine. Significantly, the 'Benz' plate on the German-engined productions was replaced with 'McClaren-Benz' on the units made in Leeds.

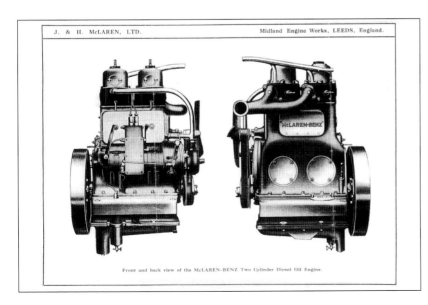

Front and back view of the McLAREN-BENZ Two Cylinder Diesel Oil Engine.

McClaren-Benz oil tractor

Engine: McClaren-Benz airless, solid injection, 4-stroke diesel oil engine with optional airstarting gear
Power: 30 brake hp at normal speed of 800rpm and capable of 10 per cent overload
Cylinders: twin 135 x 200mm bore and stroke
Governor: centrifugal, regulating the engine speed independent of the load, from 250rpm to 800rpm, with foot and screw control
Cooling: water circulating pump, fan and radiator
Fuel tank: 13 imperial gallons capacity
Clutch: adjustable plate clutch, with clutch stop
Gears forward: 3 (2, 3, 6½mph)
Gears reverse: 1 (3mph)
Springs: semi-elliptical spring to front axle
Belt Drive: pulley driven off gearbox
Steering: Achermann
Differential: Gear with locking device
Brake: hand strap brake
Weight: Shipping—60cwts (275cu ft)

Above left: A Benz Sendling 30hp tractor, circa 1927. Owned by Norman Bates.

A view of the left and right sides of the McClaren-Benz 2-cylinder oil engine. *(Courtesy Henry Roskilly, whose grandfather was a design engineer for J and H McClaren Ltd.)*

FOWLER REIN DRIVE

Although produced by John Fowler and Company Ltd of Leeds, England, the Rein Drive was designed by Cornelius Murname of Melbourne, Australia, in 1923. Despite winning a gold medal at the Royal Agricultural Show at Leicester in 1924, the Rein Drive was one of Fowler's few failures. The Fowler board thought that being able to drive the tractor with a pair of reins would win over farmers, who were hesitant to replace the familiarity of a pair of reins with such complexities as a steering wheel, clutch and gear levers. However, sales failed to materialise. Possibly the daunting prospect of controlling the big vee twin 32hp engine, with its 5.75 x 7.5in bore and stroke, by means of only a rope, turned many potential buyers away. It should be noted that the German-made Borsig tractor of 1927 also featured reins, as did a number of small production-run American tractors, including the Line Drive from Wisconsin.

This rare Fowler Rein Drive artefact is on display at the Pioneer Park Museum, Parkes, Australia.

THE FOWLER REIN DRIVE TRACTOR, WITH 2 TON TRUCK.
SHOWING ARRANGEMENT OF SPECIAL HARVESTER DRIVE.

TRACTOR HAULING 7-TON LOAD.

Top: An interesting picture of a Rein Drive attached to a trailer. Note the power take-off drive to the belt pulley.

Bottom: This photo illustrates the ability of the 2 ton, 2-wheeled tractor to pull a combined load of 7 tons. Note the operator riding in the cart controlling the tractor with a pair of reins.

Acknowledgements

I wish to express my sincere gratitude to all those who have contributed to the creation of *The Magic of Old Tractors*. I include here my tractor mates who have been more than generous with their suggestions and contributions of information, my publisher and her team, whose enthusiasm for the project inspired me to 'get on with it', plus the thousands of tractor folk around the world who have purchased my previous works and thus given me encouragement to continue writing. But especially I wish to thank my wife Margery. Without her computer skills, her endless support and her beautiful love, there simply would not have been a book.

Index

Note: Page numbers in **bold** refer to detailed
  information contained in captions. Page
  numbers in *italics* refer to illustrations.

acid rain 102
Adams, HW 78
air compressors **48**
Alderman, Alvin *144*
Allgaier R22 52, *52*
Allis Chalmers
  6-12 Motor Cultivator *148*, **149**
  B model 51, 52, *52*
  B/C series sales 124
  Model U *174*
Allis Chalmers Manufacturing Company **46**
Allrad Acker Bulldog *112*
Anderson, Vern and Grace *142*, *152*
anecdotes
  Fordson/Lanz demonstration 70–73
  Moline Universal trade-in 39–40
  night ploughing mishap 24–26
  rabbit warren clearing 165–69
  submerged Bulldog 130–31, *131*
Arbuckle, Stephen *140*
AS Hydor, Denmark **48**
Athens Plow Company, Ohio 173
Atkins, Eric *123*
Aultman Taylor 30-60 tractors 75, *75*
Australian Special, Hart Parr models 183
Avery 12-25
  1912 advertisement *17*
  performance 16

backhoes
  JCB 3C loader *49*
  MF 710 47cap
  Whitlock 60-66 loader 49
Bailor tractors 54, *54*
Bamber, Herbert 90
Batchelor, B and T *15*
Bates, Norman *185*
battery, 6-volt 38
Becker, Colin *81*
belt hp 16, 18
Benjamin, Bert 148
Benz Sendling 30hp tractor *185*
Bethelson, Dave *156*
Big 4 legend 22–23
Biggs, Luke B 182
'blindfold navigation' competition *12*
BMB President 53, *53*
BMC Mini 120–23, *121*, *122*, *123*
Bolwell, Eric *137*
Bone, Bob *35*
Boothmac grader *45*

brake hp 18
brakes
  double-disc 127
  Farmall F12 ?? **149**
Breda
  1949 crawler *103*
  50 D model 103
  70 D model 103
  50 SD model 103, *104*
  50 SD schematic drawing *104*
Brimblecombe, Ab 62, 66
Brinkmann, Mal *173*
Bristol 20 crawler 54, *54*
British Anzani Iron Horse engine 138, *138*
British Motor Corporation (BMC) 120
British Standard Machinery Company **47**
Britstand bulldozer *47*
Brown, David 159
Bruns, Al *132*
Burly cattle property, Australia 165–72
Burns, Les 82

cable winch plough 86, *86*
Caldwell Vale 80hp, transport version *43*
Cameron, Graham *43*
Cameron, Mal *40*, 56, 58
carburettors
  3-bowl 38, *41*
  Higgins 34–35, *36*
Case
  15-27, 1923 model 165–66
  25-45 Crossmount model 75, *75*
  12-20 Crossmount tractor *45*
  15-27 model *166*
  Crossmount advertisement *76*
  LA model 166–68, *167*
  Model C, 1937 *14*
  S-EX model 55, *55*
Caterpillar 10 crawler 55, *55*
Chaeside Loader *46*
Chamberlain
  Champion *48*
  Champion 6G *178*
  40K 140, *140*
  Super 90 77, *77*
Clayton 40 Chain Rail 76, *76*
Clayton Shuttleworth Ltd 104
Clements, Tony 67
Cleveland Motor Plow **181**
Cochran, Jack 78, *150*
Cockshutt 90 77, *77*
collectors 11–13
Commonsense 20-50 78, *78*
Conquip 6-ton mobile crane *49*
cooling systems, oil 34–35

CO-OP 3 78, *78*
CO-OP 2 Row Crop *150*
Coventry Victor engine bay *64*
cranes
  Conquip 6-ton mobile *49*
  Fordson *46*
crawlers
  1920 Renault GP *157*
  airfield duties 159–60
  Breda 103, *103*, *104*
  Bristol 20 54, *54*
  Caterpillar 10 55, *55*
  David Brown 50 TD 74
  David Brown 30T *164*
  Fowler VF 139, *140*
  half-track configuration *110*
  Hanomag K50 81, *81*
  Hanomag K55 47
  Holt Caterpillar 45 81, *81*
  HSCS L25 *106*
  increasing demand 111
  Lanz problems *132*, 134
  Lanz T *135*
  Nord ADN 25 *64*, 65, *65*
  Platypus 30 *184*
  Renault GP 139, *157*
  roadless half tracks *110*, 176–77
  Stock Raupenstock 68, *68*
  trackmasters 162, *163*
cropmasters 161, 161–62, *162*
Cushing, Bart *8*, *151*

Dain *33*
Daniels family *44*
Dass, Billy *161*
David Brown
  50 TD crawler 74
  Cropmaster 162
  serial numbers prefixes *164*
  30T *164*
  Taskmaster *163*
  Taskmaster transmission housing *164*
  Trackmaster *164*
  unusual early features 163
  VAD Cropmaster 161
  VAK 1 159–60
  VAK 1A 160, *161*
  VAK 1C Cropmaster 161, *161*
  VIG, aircraft towing **163**
David Brown Tractors Limited 159–61
Daw, Margery *49*
Desch, Peter 81
Deutz
  D25 model *141*, 141–42
  F3M 417 model 79, *79*

diesel fuel *143*
Dingo Creek, Wingham Australia *14*
Dissinger, 1904 model 22
'distillate' *10*
drawbar hp 16
drawbar pull 16–17
drive configurations
   3 all-wheel 28–29, *30, 33*
   3-wheel principle 32
Dutra D4 KB 79, *79*
Dyke, Les 128

Egelmeers, Jan *119*
Ehlerding, Dan **19**, *39, 75*
Ehlerding, Howard 39–40
Eicher EM 200 56, *56*
Emerson, Ralph 27
Emerson Brantingham
   Big 4 23–26, *25, 27*
   Big 4-30 *23*
   Q 12-20, 1920 model *19, 19*
   tractor models *24*
Emerson Brantingham Implement Company,
   Illinois 23, *27*
Empire 88 57, *57*
engines
   1-cylinder full compression ignition diesel
     139, 140
   1-cylinder petrol 138, *138*
   1-cylinder semidiesel 92–95, 101, 102, 139,
     139
   2-cylinder diesel 141–42
   2-cylinder petrol–kerosene 140
   2-stroke crude oil burner *107*
   3-cylinder diesel 142, *143*
   4-cylinder diesel 102, 144
   4-cylinder ohv pressure lubricated 38
   4-cylinder petrol–kerosene *143*, 143–44
   6-cylinder diesel 146–47
   6-cylinder petrol–kerosene 146
   Bamber's 90
   BMC Mini 120–22, *122*, 123
   Breda 50 SD 103
   Continental S10 175
   Coventry Victor *64*
   design evolution 22–23
   distinctive sounds 101
   Farmall Regular 149
   first V8 use 78
   Fowler 119
   HSCS *105*
   hybrid steam traction 22
   Ivel tractor *64*
   John Deere D **18**
   Junkers 103
   Lanz-type semidiesel 93
   Marshall 91cap, 93, 119
   McClaren-Benz *185*
   Nord ADN 25 *64*
   offset position *41*
   Oliver Super 55 *126, 127*
   postwar Field Marshall series 93

postwar O&K 99
1950s designs 138–47
Saunderson Elstow 4-cylinder *33*
Super Landini *109*
Eron D 56, *56*

Fate Root Heath Company 182–83
Ferguson
   promotional material *58*
   TE series 51, 120, 127–28
   TEA 20 model *169*, 171
   TED 57, *57*
   TO 20 model 124
   TO series 51, 127–28
   Type A 159, *160*
Ferguson, Harry 120, 159
Fiat 80R 80, *80*
Field Marshall Series 3A 95, *95, 96*
Fitch Four-Drive Model D4 *43*
Flett, Bill 48
Flower, James 53
Forbes, Fay 134
Ford
   3000 model *49*
   9N model 58, *58*
Ford, Roy 46
Fordson
   composite picture *45*
   E27N *46*
   Major Diesel, 1955 model *73*
   Major Diesel demonstration 70–73
   Major E27N roadless half track 176–77, *177*
   Model F 42, *50*, 173, *173*
   N All Around row cropper *153*
   Power Major *49*
   Super Major *48*
Four-Drive Tractor Company **43**
Fowler
   rein drive 186, *186, 187*
   VF crawler engine 139, *140*
Francis, Col *156*
friction drive 175–76
Froelich 80, *80*
front-end loaders
   advent of 42
   early 176
   MF 702 **47**
   Whitlock 60-66 model *48*
fuels 10, 101, 109cap, *130, 143*

Gas Traction Company, Minneapolis 23
Gas Traction Company Big 4-30 23
gasoline *10*
gear trains *17*
Glasgow tractor *30*
Goldsworthy, R and C *154*
Gospal, Gib 47
graders
   Boothmac *45*
   Patrol *46*
Graham Bradley row cropper *152*
Gray S 18-36, 1920 model 20, *20*

Guldner AF 30 59, *59*
Guthrie, William **30**

half-track equipment *110*, 176–77
Hanomag
   advertisement 150
   K50 crawler 81, *81*
   K55 crawler *47*
   large vintage collection 81
   R27 Row Crop 150, *150*
   R35 Row Crop 150, *150*
Harbin, Jack *180*
Harris, Alanson *183*
Harris, Peter *151*
Harry Ferguson Research Ltd 120
Harry Ferguson Tractor Club Australasia Inc *51*
Hart Parr 18-36 tractor 183, *184*
Hart Parr Company, Iowa 183
Hartsough, DM 22
Hawkins, David *174*
Heider Manufacturing Company, Iowa 21
Heider Rock Island 15-27, 1925 model 21, *21*
Heinrich Lanz AG, Germany 51, 105, 115, 150
heritage items, tractors as 28, 179
'Hi Crop' tractors 154
Higgins carburettor 34–35, 36
Hill, Merv *163, 164*
Hindman, Johnny 170
hoarders 12
Hofherr-Schrantz-Clayton-Shuttleworth
   see HSCS
Holt Caterpillar
   45 crawler 81, *81*
   tractors 44
horsepower
   Bamber/horse comparison 90
   basics 16
   calculations 18
   comparison of characteristics 19–21
   heavyweight tractors 74
Howard
   DH 22 tractor 59, *59, 184*
   Trench Digger and Pipe Layer *184*
Howard, Arthur Clifford *184*
HSCS
   company history 104–5, **106**
   engine *105*
   G35 *106*
   K40 or K50 *101*
   L25 crawler *106*
   R30-35 *107*
   Steel horse 105
Huber
   22-38 model *74*, 82, *82*
   1898 model 22
Huber, Dr Fritz 105, 112, 129, 130, *131*, 137
Huber, Hansludwig 137
Hughes, Barry 46
Hungerford, Ross 52
Hydor A105 *48*
hydraulic circuitry, Vickers 127
hydraulic power technology 42–43

ignition switch keys *41*
indicated hp 18
industrial applications 42–50
Innes, Ferg *106*
International
 Farmall A model *13*, 124
 Farmall F12 60, *60*, 149, *149*
 Farmall M model *154*
 Farmall Regular 149
 Farmall Super A *60*, 61, *61*
 Friction Drive 175, *176*
 Mogul Type C *44*
 Titan Type D 82, *82*
International Harvester Company 148
International McCormick
 Deering O4 model 144
 Deering W4 Standard *143*, 143–44, *144*
 A model 51
 Super AWD6 *12*, *19*
 WD6 16–17
Ivel tractor 61, *61*, *64*

J and H McClaren Ltd, Leeds, England 185
JCB 3C loader backhoe *49*
Jensen, Wayne and Bob 61
JI Case Company, Wisconsin 23, 27
John Deere
 402 disc plough *13*
 420 Hi Crop *154*
 BR model, 1935 *8*
 Dain *33*
 early Model D 83, *83*
 GPWT *151*
 Model AR, 1948 *13*
 Model D 16–17, *18*, 83, *83*
 Model L 62, *62*
 takes over Lanz 137
Johnston, Ian M *123*, *172*
 company vehicle *72*
 jackaroo experience 165–72
 Leeton demonstration 70–73
 private collection 52, 63, 80, 84, 85, 94, *98*, *99*,
 100, *125*, *145*, *149*, *154*, *162*, *177*, *178*
Johnston, Norm *23*, *25*

Kahl, L 55
Keech, Ron 79
Kelly and Lewis (KL) Ltd 108, 133–36
Kemp, Warren and Rodney *106*
Kennedy, Bruce 137
kerosene 10
'Kerosene Annie' 34
Kick, Stan *96*
Kindred Haines, 1901 model 22
Kirkpatrick, John 86
KL Bulldog
 1949 model *14*
 advertisement *136*
 product history 108, 118, 135–37
Kurtz family *167*
Laing, L *164*
Lake Goldsmith Rally, Australia *51*

'lamp oil' 10
Landini
 advertisement *110*
 Bufalo *111*
 Cv 35-40 model *110*
 Cv 55-60 model *110*, 111
 engine *109*
 L25 model *110*
 Super Landini *109*, 111
Landini, Giovanni 109, 111
Lanyon, Evan *13*
Lanz
 15-30 model 92
 12-20 Row Crop Bulldog *154*
 branch service depots 118–19
 Bull Model T (D6006) 83, *83*
 Bulldog 15, *113*
 Bulldog 1939 55hp *112*
 Bulldog copies 108, 118–19
 Bulldog D1706 63, *63*
 Bulldog D2416 (Model H) *114*, *115*
 Bulldog D3606 70–73, *72*, *73*
 Bulldog design improvements 102
 Bulldog HL 112, *115*
 Bulldog HR 8 (Model P) *114*
 Bulldog Model H *71*
 Bulldog Model Q engine 139, *139*
 Bulldogs in Russia 130–31, *131*
 crawler problems *132*, 134
 T crawler *135*
 Type HN Dreirad-Hackfrucht-
 Bulldog 150
Lanz Australia Pty Ltd 70
Latimore, Alan 62, *169*
Leyland 154 tractor 123
LHB Model LH 5 tractor 62, *62*
lightweight tractors 51–69, 120–23
Lyons, Patrick 22–23

M Rumely Company, Indiana 34
Malcolm Moore
 cable loader 175–76, *177*
 electric welder *50*
Malcolm Moore & Company, Australia **50**
Malcolm Moore Industries Ltd, Australia 175
Malloch, RA *88*
Marshall
 12-20 model *94*, 94–95
 15-30 model 92
 18-30 model *92*, 93–94
 Colonial Class C 91
 Colonial Class D 91
 Colonial Class E 91, *91*
 Colonial Class F *90*, 91
 Colonial Class G 91
 Colonial production history *90*, 90–91, *91*
 Field Marshall series *95*, 95
 MP6 *96*, 96–97, *97*
 MP4 prototype **96**
Martin, Jesse 82, *96*
Massey Ferguson
 710 backhoe **47**

702 front-end loader **47**
88 model 84, *84*
Workbull 47
Massey Ferguson Ltd *183*
Massey Harris
 25 model 84, *84*, *85*
 30 model *13*, *151*
 203 model 85, *85*
 744 PD 146–47, *147*
 3-4 Plow 84
 Pacemaker 85
Massey Harris Company Ltd *183*
maximum hp 18
McClaren Diesel Oil-Engined Windlass 86, *86*
McClaren-Benz oil tractor 185, *185*
McClelland, Andy 83
McCormick 15-30 88
McDermott, Dudley and Dianne 59
McDonald
 EA model 116
 EB model 86, *86*
 TWB 116, *116*, *117*, 118
 TX Super Diesel 116
McDonald, Alfred Henry 116, 118
McDonald, Neal 116, *116*, 118
McKenzie, B and N *146*
McKenzie, Norm 61, *184*
mineral oil 101
Minneapolis Moline Co. **153**
Moline
 RTU row cropper *153*
 Universal 38
 Universal Model D 38, *40*, *41*
Moline Plow Company 38
Moree, Australia 170–71
Morrell, T Herbert 124–25, 128, 146
Morris Isis *72*
Mort's Dock Ltd 181
Munich Machinery Museum opening *15*
Murr, Alios 129–37, *135*
Muscat, Fred *153*

naphtha oil, crude 101, **109**
New Zealand Special, Hart Parr models 183
Newman AN 3 tractor 63, *63*, *64*
Noll, Les 65, *176*
Nord ADN 25 tractor *64*, 65, *65*

O'Brien, Pat *46*, *95*
O'Connor, Bill *49*
'oil pull' technology 34
Oliver
 60 Row Crop *152*
 Standard Fleetline 88 146, *146*
 Super 55 124–28, *125*, *126*, *127*
Oliver Farm Equipment Corporation 183
orchard tractor, custom-built 20
Orenstein & Koppel conglomeration 98–100
Orenstein & Koppel S32K 98, *98*, 99–100, *100*
OTA Monarch 65, *65*
over-loaders 42

Pain, Trevor *182*
Pampa Bulldog *119*
paraffin 10
Parliament building, Australian *49*
Parrett, Dent 78, **150**
Patrol grader *46*
Pawley, Joshua M **44**
Payne, John and Merna *103*
performance figures *see* horsepower
petrol 10
Pettith, Mick *12, 19*
Pink, Craig *137*
pioneers, early 22
piston speed *174*
Platypus 30 Crawler *184*
ploughs
  3-furrow 28, *29*
  4-furrow 28
  8-furrow mouldboard *35*
  John Deere 402 disc *13*
  Squire Auto Plough 180–81, *181*
  'stump jump' 117
Plunkett, Andy *44*
Plymouth/Silver King tractors 182–83
Porsche Standard Star 66, *66*
power take off (pto) hp 18
President tractors 53, *53*
Pryor, Howard 68
Puls, Barbara 65
Puls, Darren *139*
Puls, Mark *140*
Purcell Engineering Company Ltd 180

rabbit warrens, tearing out 165–69
RAC hp 18
Radnidge, Bob *14*
rare tractors
  1920 Gray S 18-36 21
  1918 Ruggles & Parsons 12-20 *15*
  Eron D 56, *56*
  Fiat 80R 80, *80*
  Fitch Four-Drive Model D4 *43*
  Fowler Rein Drive *186*
  Marshall 18-30 *92*
  McDonald 1912 EB 86, *86*
  OTA Monarch 65, *65*
  Saunderson Type A 31
  S32K 98, 99–100, *100*
  Wallis Bear 89, *89*
rated hp 18
Red Star Tractors **106**
rein drive, Fowler 186, *186, 187*
Renault
  1949 advertisement *157*
  1920 GP *157*
  3042 model 155, *156*
  3042 specifications *158*
  PE model *156*
Richardson, Burly Bill 165, 168–70, 172
Richardson, Mrs 165, 168–69, 172
road tractors *112*
roadless half tracks **110**, 176–77

Robertson, Ian M 78, *91*
Rock Island Plow Company, Illinois 21
Rosenboom family *149*
Roseworthy Agricultural College, South
  Australia 28, *29*
Ross-Reid, John 70–73, *71*
row croppers 148–54
Ruggles & Parsons 12-20, 1918 model *15*
Ruhl, Athol *177*
Rumely
  Do All 66, *66*
  Oil Pull 25-40 Model B 34
  Oil Pull 30-60 Model E *36*
  Oil Pull 30-66 Model E 34, *35*
  Oil Pull 15-30 Model F 34, *35, 37*

Sainsbury, Brian *18*
Same 12 HP 67, *67*
Sanders, Bill and Stuart 79
Sanders, Freeman 144
Sandstone Estates, South Africa 178–79, *179*
Sanger, Ted 59, 67
Saunderson Type A *29*
  1907 brochure *31*
  1908 model *31*
  rear view *32*
  restoration 29
  South Australian interest 28–30
Schmidt, EF 89
Schuster, Reg *43*
Scouller, Catherine 54
Shaw, H and G 56
Sheat, Noel *45*
Sheppard Diesel SD3 142, *142,* **143**
Sift TD 4 87, *87*
Silver King R44 *182,* 182–83
Simon, Ludwig 70–73, *72*
S32K 98, *98,* 99–100, *100*
Smith, Les *153*
Smith, Sir Keith *88*
Spittle, GH *139*
Squire
  Auto Plough 180–81, *181*
  Quad Drive 180, *180*
Squire, Fred *180*
Squire, Raimond Ash *180,* 180–81
Squire, Ron *181*
starter igniters, making *175*
starting procedures
  Big 4 *25*
  HSCS L25 **106**
  KL Bulldog *108*
statistics
  1957 exports 179
  1957 tractor populations 179
steering
  automatic 25, *26*
  chain windlass *35*
  Dreadnought Guide Self Steer *35*
Steyr 80 67, *67*
Stihl 144 68, *68*
Stock Raupenstock crawler 68, *68, 69*

Sultana, Peter 56

Tail End Charlie *178*
takeover bids 128
tar fuel *130*
36-PS-Diesel-Kompressor-Schlepper-S32K
  see S32K
Thomas, Mel 87
Thornton, Max 83
trackmasters 162, *163*
traction 16–17, 31
tractor events 11, *12, 13, 14, 19, 51*
'tractor' name, origin 183
Transit Thresher Company, Minneapolis 23
'transport' tractors
  Caldwell Vale *43*
  Lanz Bulldog 1939 55hp *112*
tricycle configuration 150, 153
Tronser, Hans *132,* 133–34, 135, 137, *137*
Turner Yeoman of England
  engine 144, *145*
  restored *145*
Twin City 27-44 tractor 87, *87*
tyres
  pneumatic 16, 42
  solid rubber 42

United tractor 174–75
Universal Tractor Manufacturing Company,
  Ohio 38
Ursus Bulldog 118–19, *119*
utility tractors 123, 124

'vaporising oil' 10
Vickers 15-30 88, *88*
vintage tractor events *13, 14, 19*

Wallis Bear 89, *89*
Wallis Cub Junior model J 69, *69*
Watt, James 18
welding equipment, electric *50*
wheel slip 16–17, 31
Whitlock
  66 Loader *48*
  60-66 loader backhoe *49*
William Marshall Sons & Company 90
Williams, Newton 28, *29,* 30, 87
world records, Guinness 178–79

Xaver Fendt, Germany 51

Yates, David 63